THEORIES OF PERSONALITY

THEORIES OF PERSONALITY
A Systems Approach

David Lester
The Richard Stockton College of New Jersey

Taylor & Francis
Publishers since 1798

USA	Publishing Office:	Taylor & Francis 1101 Vermont Ave., N.W., Suite 200 Washington, DC 20005 Tel: (202) 289-2174 Fax: (202) 289-3665
	Distribution Center:	Taylor & Francis 1900 Frost Road, Suite 101 Bristol, PA 19007-1598 Tel: (215) 785-5800 Fax: (215) 785-5515
UK		Taylor & Francis, Ltd. 4 John Street London WC1N 2ET Tel: 071 405 2237 Fax: 071 831 2035

THEORIES OF PERSONALITY: A Systems Approach

1 2 3 4 5 6 7 8 9 0 BRBR 0 9 8 7 6 5

This book was set in Times Roman by Harlowe Typography, Inc.. The editors was Joyce Duncan. Cover design by Michelle Fleitz. Printing and binding by Braun-Brumfield, Inc.

A CIP catalog record for this book is available from the British Library.

∞ The paper in this publication meets the requirements of the ANSI Standard Z39.48-1984 (Permanence of Paper)

Library of Congress Cataloging-in-Publication Data
Lester, David,
   Theories of personality: a systems approach/David Lester.
     p. cm.
   Includes bibliographical references and index.

   1. Personality. I. Title.
BF696.L3975 1995
155.2—dc20

                             95-19902
                             CIP

ISBN 1-56032-350-7 (cloth)
ISBN 1-56032-351-5 (paper)

Contents

II
THEORIES BASED ON COGNITION

**4   George Kelly's Personal Construct Theory:
      A Theory of Cognition**   **41**

IV
CONCLUSIONS

Preface

This book is designed as a supplementary text for undergraduate students and graduate students taking a course on theories of personality. This raises the question, therefore, of why a supplementary text is needed for this topic in psychology.

My aims in this book are (1) to present intrapsychic theories of personality in a modern, rational manner, and (2) to show that the multitude of theories presented in standard textbooks are not independent theories, but rather can be seen as alternative ways of presenting a few basic ideas.

Textbooks that cover theories of personality have become increasingly uniform in recent years. In order to appeal to as wide an audience as possible, textbook writers and publishers are reluctant to espouse a particular point of view, for to do so might discourage instructors from adopting the book. For a similar reason, textbook writers and publishers have restricted themselves to a standard presentation of each theorist, so that each new textbook (or revision of an older textbook) looks as if it has been cut and pasted from the other two dozen textbooks already on the market. (Indeed, I sometimes doubt that an author has read the theorist's original works!)

This would be satisfactory, at least for me, if I agreed with the uniform style of the textbooks on theories of personality. But this is not the case. I have found, therefore, that, disliking one, I dislike them all. My own viewpoint, evolved over the many years that I have taught this course, deviates to a considerable extent from the way in which the theories are presented in the textbooks. Let me give a few examples.

Almost every textbook I have previewed, included those I have chosen to use for my course, presents Freud's theory of personality in an archaic form. Freud is presented as Freud wrote the theory. My objection is that I am not teaching a course on the history of psychology. There have been recent, and more rational, presentations of the material. Thus, as an instructor, I have to tell the students to read the chapter on Freud in their text, but to pay more attention to my lectures. On the other hand, on examinations, I have to give credit for the archaic definitions of Freudian terms since they are in the textbook that the students read, as well as giving credit to those who have understook the definitions of the terms as I have given them in my lectures.

I have similar problems with the way other theorists are presented. George Kelly chose to present his theory as if it were a mathematical model, with postulates and corollaries. Most textbook writers follow this format. I object. If we think that a formal, logical model of presentation is useful, then all the chapters should be presented in that style. If we think it is not useful, then Kelly's theory should be presented as are the other theories. Again, "Theories of Personality" is *not* a "History of Psychology" course. To take an analogy, modern textbooks on physics do not present Newton's ideas in the form in which they were presented in *Philosophiae Naturalis Principia Mathematica* in 1687. They are presented, where appropriate, in a modern form.

My preferred format for presenting the various theories of personality has evolved over time, but to write a textbook organized around these ideas would depart considerably from the uniformity demanded of textbooks, and so the presentation of these ideas in a brief supplementary book seemed more appropriate.

This book, as a result, deviates from the contents of most textbooks on theories of personality. As I have already hinted, the presentation of some of the theorists does *not* follow the conventional format. Rather, I have tried to present more rational versions of the theories, sometimes discussing what the theorists "ought" to have said alongside what they actually said.

The book is structured around the three major theorists in the field of personality: Sigmund Freud, George Kelly, and Andras Angyal. In each of the three parts, the views of the major theorist are presented in one chapter, and variations on these views are presented in the following chapter.

Why then do three chapters follow the chapter on Andras Angyal? As I began to organize this volume, I found that holistic views in theories of personality were quite common, much more common than the major textbooks appear to realize. Indeed, holistic ideas can be found even in those theorists I have labeled at "atomistic." After all, Kelly's notion of a "construction system" (see Chapter 4) is a holistic concept.

As I surveyed these alternative holistic views, I found that they separated into three major areas: (a) theorists who have focused on the split in the mind between the real self and the ideal self, (b) recent theorists who have explored the possibility that the mind is a "multiplicity of selves," and (c) theorists who have a holistic viewpoint which is not sufficiently articulated so that it provides a basis for explaining human behavior in detail, but who are well established in the history of psychology. In order to provide a clearer presentation of these three areas, I assigned each to a separate chapter. A final chapter draws conclusions from the material presented.

1

Introduction

There are three major approaches to the explanation of human behavior. The present volume is concerned with *intrapsychic explanations*, explanations that use concepts based on psychological processes and "structures" within the mind. These explanations may focus on the contents of the mind, such as the existence of particular desires, emotions or thoughts, but typically define and utilize more complicated processes and structures such as "defense mechanisms," "complexes," and "system principles."

A second approach also focuses on the individual, but rather than using mental processes to explain human behavior, relies on the physiology of the brain. Willliam Sheldon and Hans Eysenck have proposed classic *physiological theories* of personality, and recent advances in biological psychiatry look as if they may form the basis for modern improved physiological theories of personality.

The third approach focuses on the environment (or the situation) of the individual as the source of explanations for human behavior. *Simple learning theory*, originally proposed by Edward Thorndike (1874–1949), Edwin Guthrie (1886–1958) and Clark Hull (1884–1952), but more recently associated with B. F. Skinner, illustrates one version of this approach. *Social learning theory* takes into account the fact that humans are more complex than lower animals, and introduces a limited number of intrapsychic processes (mainly cognitive elements) in order to provide a more complete explanation of human behavior. The theories proposed by Albert Bandura and Julian Rotter are good examples of this approach.

It is a truism that the final answer to most questions is a combination of the many different answers that have been proposed. Therefore, human behavior in general is probably best explained by a combination of these three different approaches. However, psychology has typically advanced by individuals first proposing extreme versions of the more limited domain theories, followed by others who subsequently integrate these rival theories into a fuller explanation.

Over the years, the particular theories of human behavior that are included in a textbook on theories of personality have grown to include almost all explanations of human behavior. Yet college courses are still taught on topics, such as learning, physiological psychology, and social psychology, that cover the biological and situational explanations of human behavior comprehensively. The question that arises, therefore, is what unique material should be covered in a course on theories of personality. The choice for this volume is the intrapsychic theories.

Many textbooks start by listing varying definitions of the term "personality," including both the standard dictionary definitions and those proposed by psychologists over the years. A popular one comes from Allport (1961, p. 28): "Personality is the dynamic organization within the individual of those psychophysical systems that determine his characteristic behavior and thought," a definition that falls clearly into the intrapsychic perspective. Personality is concerned with processes *within* the individual's mind.

With what general phenomena are theories of personality concerned? First, a theory of personality tries to explain why our attitudes, goals, and, to a lesser extent, our behavior are consistent over time. We behave repeatedly in similar ways, and this could be a result of our psychological processes or structures being stable over time. Second, we behave quite differently from others, and this could be because our psychological processes and structures differ from theirs. The concepts of intrapsychic theories of personality explain both phenomena.

HOW MANY INTRAPSYCHIC THEORIES ARE THERE?

When I first came to the study of theories of personality, I was surprised to find that my student textbook apparently contained more than two dozen theories. Instead of conveying a sense of the richness of psychological thought, this led to skepticism on my part that so many different theories could possibly exist. I stifled my doubts, read my textbook, passed my qualifying examination, and later taught the course myself. But after a few years, I decided that I had to "forget" all that I had learned and begin afresh to look at the topic. As part of this process, I read the seminal works of each personality theorist.

I focused on the fact that psychological processes have been divided into one of the three types, depending on whether they focus on desires, thoughts, or emotions (commonly called *conation*, *cognition*, and *affect*, respectively). There were theories of personality that focused on desires (Freud's psychoanalytic theory, for example) and theories that focused on thoughts (Kelly's personal construct theory, for example), but none that focused on emotions. Although some psychologists have tried to bring emotions into explanations of personality (e.g., Plutchik, 1962), the efforts have not been as comprehensive as those based on desires and on thoughts.

The decision as to which are the most comprehensive theories of personality based on desires and on thinking is, of course, subjective. I have chosen Freud's psychoanalytic theory as the most comprehensive theory of personality based on desires and Kelly's personal construct theory for thinking. These theories have assumed major importance in all textbooks on personality, and I think that both provide more explanatory concepts and, therefore, more explanatory power than other theories of personality based on desires and thoughts.

For Kelly, it was necessary to read his published works. But for Freud, the question arises of whether to read Freud's original writings or to focus on some of the more modern works in psychoanalysis. Two considerations shaped my choice. The first was that, obviously, Freud began writing over a century ago, and so lacked the knowledge that is available to a contemporary psychologist.

Thus, his original works are more relevant to the history of psychology than to psychology today. An interesting question to ask is how would Freud have written his theory if he were writing it today? The second consideration that shaped my choice was meeting a contemporary psychoanalyst, Walter Toman, and being tremendously impressed by the opening paragraph of his book on psychoanalysis. As an undergraduate in England, I had first studied physics and mathematics before switching to psychology. Furthermore, the types of psychology covered at my university were almost all "experimental psychology," that is, learning theory, sensation and perception, and physiological psychology. I came to America, therefore, with a low opinion of such areas as personality. Freud's psychoanalytic theory, in particular, struck me as, dare I admit it now, nonsense. Ids, egos, and superegos seemed to me to be like cartoon characters, unrealistic gnomes fighting battles with one another. In the first paragraph of his book, Toman noted that the basic elements of psychoanalytic theory are psychological forces, with desires being the most common. He said that we can distinguish three subsets of desires—the id, the ego, and the superego. In an instant, my conception of psychoanalytic theory was transformed. An id was not a real object; it was instead a particular subset of a larger field of objects. It should be used as an adjective, not as a noun. The id did not exist, but id desires might.

I was also fortunate in studying under George Kelly, which admittedly might have biased me in favor of choosing his theory as the most comprehensive theory of personality based on thinking. How to incorporate *holistic* ideas into theories of personality was a more subjective decision. As we will see later in this volume, many theorists have proposed holistic concepts in personality, that is, they have stressed that the mind is an organized and dynamic whole and that an analysis of the mind's component parts (individual desires and thoughts) will never provide a complete picture. Who has provided the most comprehensive holistic theory?

Again serendipity played a role in my choice. When I met him, Abraham Maslow no longer taught graduate students, only undergraduates. So I took an undergraduate course with him and became his teaching assistant. Because of these experiences, and other personal encounters, I was strongly influenced by him. In particular, he introduced me to the writings of Andras Angyal, a theorist who is often omitted from contemporary textbooks on personality. However, when I reread Angyal's books, I realized that his theory was extraordinarily comprehensive, although it was rather technical and lacked good concrete examples of some of the processes described.

I then had the basis for my thinking on personality:

the atomistic perspective:
 desires/wishes: Freud's psychoanalytic theory
 thoughts/cognitions: Kelly's personal construct theory
 emotions: no theory
the holistic perspective: Angyal's theory

The remaining task was now clear. As I read each new theorist, all I had to do was asked myself one question. Where have I came across this idea before—

in Freud, Kelly, or Angyal? And if the answer was that I had not come across the idea before, then I had a new principle, process, or structure. How many new principles, processes, and structures would I find?

To anticipate the answer, I can say that I found only one. I found many different ways of expressing the same idea first described by Freud, Kelly, or Angyal. I found many different proposals for the material contents of the psychological structures proposed by Freud, Kelly, and Angyal. I found theorists who extended and expanded upon the ideas expressed by the three seminal theorists. But I found only one new principle—the principle of balance described by Carl Jung, wherein each complex in the mind must be balanced by a complementary complex.

I was able to teach my course on theories of personality contentedly. Instead of some two dozen rival theories of personality, there were three basic theories of personality and many variants on these three themes.

Remember that claims of who first proposed a concept or a principle is not of concern here. Rather than historic precedence, I am concerned with who formulated the concept best and incorporated it into the most comprehensive theory. Frequently, the formulation of an idea by another theorist has become more popular or been more stimulating than that made by Freud, Kelly, or Angyal. For example, Carl Roger's writing on the conditions of worth imposed on the child by parents, which leads to the child's real self being suppressed, have become a much more popular set of terms than Angyal's pattern of vicarious living. Or, to take another example, Festinger's theory of cognitive dissonance has generated far more research than Kelly's concept of hostility. However, in this volume, having chosen Angyal and Kelly to be among the seminal theorists, the question is whether Rogers and Festinger provide new concepts, i.e., concepts not already described in the earlier chapters on Angyal and Kelly. (For Rogers and Festinger, the answer is no.)

I

THEORIES BASED ON MOTIVATION

2

Freud's Psychoanalytic Theory: A Theory About Wishes

Freud's theory was the first major modern theory of personality. Many later theories were developed by modifying some aspect of Freud's theory or by rejecting one feature and proposing a new theory that set up a dialectic with Freud's theory. As such, Freud's theory is the seminal theory of personality.

However, there are flaws in the way that the theory is presented in many textbooks. The theory as written by Freud has assumed the status of scripture. Authors usually present the theory as Freud described it. However, authors in other disciplines present older theories in the light of modern knowledge. In physics, for example, only historians of science read Newton's work, and no physics textbook presents physics in the way that Newton did. Likewise, there are modern restatements of Freud's theory that present the theory in a more systematic, and thus testable way, taking into account modern ideas about psychology. Cofer and Appley (1964), in their classic work on motivation, cite the presentations by Rapaport (1959) and Toman (1960) in particular.

UPDATING THE THEORY

Freud was a genius, perhaps the only genius who has worked in the field of psychology. (This clearly indicates my bias!) Being a genius, if he were writing today, he would not write the theory in the way that he did in the late 1800s and early 1900s. Let me give two examples.

Energizing Human Behavior

Prior to 1949, all theorists felt that they had to explain why humans showed any behavior at all. Using physics as an analogy, they believed an energy source was needed for humans to show any activity. Freud, therefore, felt called upon to propose an energy source. In his early writing he described *libido*, an energy that fueled all behavior. After observing the massive destruction of human life that occurred in the course of World War I, he proposed a second energy source, *destrudo*, which also fueled human behavior but which was destructive in orientation. Libido and destrudo, respectively, were said to energize the life and death instincts, or *eros* and *thanatos*.

In 1949, Hebb suggested that we did not need to postulate energy sources for human behavior. We could simply assume that, as long as we were alive, we would always be doing something (Hebb, 1949). The question for psychologists to answer was not why we show any behavior at all, but rather why we do this *instead of* that. Hence, theories proposed after 1949 did not propose energy sources.

Thus, Freud, had he written his theory today, might not have proposed an energy source for human behavior. Despite this, some textbooks on theories of personality continue to include a discussion of libido (and sometimes destrudo) and define it as did Freud.

Sexism

Several commentators have criticized Freud's theory for being sexist. Concepts such as *castration anxiety*, in which the little boy fears that he will be punished by castration for harboring affectionate thoughts toward his mother, are brought forward as examples of this sexism.

Of course, Freud was sexist by modern standards. However, at the time, he was considered radical and not sexist at all. To judge him by modern criteria seems unfair. Furthermore, had Freud been writing today, he probably would not have written in a sexist way. Rather than naming this anxiety in boys as castration anxiety, he might have written about *mutilation anxiety* in small children. Both boys and girls fear mutilation. For example, they hate having their hair and finger nails cut, often protesting and crying. If hospitalized, small children fear not only the separation from their parents but also the surgical mutilations that may occur. Freud's theory can easily be made non-sexist, therefore, by changing the terminology.

Translation Problems

Bettelheim (1982) pointed out that the English translators of Freud had distorted his theory in their translations, and later writers have perpetuated these errors. For example, Freud did not talk of the *mind* or psyche, but rather of the soul. He did not discuss *instincts*, but rather drives. He did not define three parts of the mind—*ego*, *id*, and *superego*—but rather the "me," the "it," and the "over-me". Giving the concepts Latin names gave them implications which the words in the original German did not have. Bettelheim gave many other examples.

Despite these criticisms, most modern presentations of Freud continue to use the terms first chosen by the translators, which perpetuates the false implications of these words.

HOW TO PRESENT FREUD'S THEORY?

How then are we to present Freud's theory of personality in a modern textbook? There have been many analyses of Freudian theory, and various ways of presenting have been tried. One modern version has been proposed by Walter Toman (1960), an Austrian psychoanalyst, who purposely tried to make Freud's theory rational from a modern point of view. He redefined the

FREUD'S LIFE

Freud was born on May 6, 1856, in the Moravian town of Freiberg, now known as Pribor in the Czech Republic. He was the first born, but the family included two older half-brothers from his father's earlier marriage (Gay, 1988). The family was Jewish in a town of 4,500 residents where 130 Jews lived. His father, a wool merchant, moved the family to Vienna. Freud showed academic promise, entering the university at age 17, but did not obtain his medical degree until he was 25. He took a junior post at Vienna General Hospital and slowly moved through the ranks. He was made a professor in 1902 after 17 years (the average length of time to achieve that rank was 8 years). He married in 1886 and eventually had six children.

His first work on psychoanalytic theory was co-authored with Joseph Breuer. Entitled *Studies in Hysteria*, it was published in 1895, 9 years after he had begun his private practice. His first book without a co-author, *The Interpretation of Dreams*, was published in 1899, when Freud was 43. Beginning in 1902, a group of interested scholars began to meet regularly at Freud's home every Wednesday to discuss the new ideas in that book and other writings. During the next 4 years Freud wrote prolifically on psychoanalysis. Thus, Freud's ideas about the theory developed in his 40s, a common age for productivity in the social sciences.

The Vienna Psychoanalytic Society was organized in 1908, with Otto Rank as the first secretary. Foreign scholars began to visit Vienna to study with Freud, and Freud began to receive honors and accolades. In 1909, Freud was awarded an honorary degree from Clark University in the United States, and in the same year the first international congress of psychoanalysts was held at Salzburg, Austria. Freud was nominated for the Nobel Prize for the first time in 1917, but to his great disappointment, he was never awarded the prize.

As he grew old, his daughter Anna began to accompany him to scholarly meetings and, eventually, to go in his place. She studied psychoanalysis (and was psychoanalyzed herself by Freud), served as her father's secretary, nurse, confidante, and colleague, and never married. After his death, Anna became an authority on children viewed from a psychoanalytic perspective. It is interesting that an Oedipal conflict should play a strong role in the life of Freud's daughter.

The rise of the National Socialist Party in Germany, and the resulting persecution of Jews, made Freud's position in Vienna precarious. Freud had collaborated on a book with William Bullitt about Woodrow Wilson, the ex-President of the United States, a book that psychoanalysts later viewed with great disfavor, omitting it from the collected works of Freud. However, Bullitt became the American ambassador to France, and he monitored Freud's status in Austria, eventually arranging for Freud to leave Germany for England in 1938 when his life seemed in danger. Ironically, a bad book played a role in saving him from death in a Nazi concentration camp.

Freud had developed cancer of the palate in 1923 and underwent some 30 operations in the ensuing years. Soon after his arrival in England the pain became unbearable and the ulcerated lesions repulsive. Freud persuaded his physician to inject him with a lethal dose of morphine, and Freud died on September 23, 1939—a physician-assisted suicide.

terms in a way that did not change their essential meaning so much as change the implications of the terms. Freud's theory will be described here using Toman's reformulation as a guide.

Many of the assumptions of Freud's theory are quite abstract, whereas others are very specific. For example, to propose that unconscious desires play a role in determining human behavior is an abstract proposition. To propose that people in general (or this person in particular) are (is) motivated in their choice of a lover or spouse by unconscious desires to be with their opposite-sex parent is a specific proposition. This specific proposition could be incorrect, either for all people or for some people, but it would not invalidate the abstract proposition that unconscious desires play a role in human behavior. Students should be careful not to reject the abstract theory if and when they reject a specific proposition.

Furthermore, journalists and writers today are hungry for quotes, and scholars are sometimes eager to be quoted. We are called all the time to comment on current events. Recently, I was called by an editorial writer for the *Lancet*, a British medical journal, to comment on why American suicide rates go down during the month of Presidential elections. I threw out some wild ideas on this and was quoted in the journal.

Psychoanalysts do the same, and sometimes, especially to the uninformed, their speculations may sound silly. For example, Dundes was interviewed by *Time* ("Football as erotic ritual," 1978) about his suggestion that American football was a homosexual ritual. Dundes noted that the uniforms are skin-tight and show the outlines of the body, including the genitals and backside, and use padding to accentuate the masculine features (such as the padded shoulders). He noted the patting of one another's backsides, holding hands, and hugging that takes place on the field. He listed the terminology used which has sexual connotations—popping an opponent or penetrating the end-zone. He compared the presentation of the backsides of the offensive linemen to the quarterback to the way that submissive monkeys present their backside to the dominant monkey who makes pelvic thrusts to prove his dominance. Finally, he mentioned that fact that football players are supposed to abstain from heterosexual activity before a game, traditionally one of the reasons teams check into hotels for the night before the game even when playing at home.

Dundes makes a strong case, and the article in *Time* presented his ideas well. Still, his scholarly article would be a better source (Dundes, 1978). It is important to remember also that his ideas are clever, scholarly fun. Rejection of his ideas does not require rejection of the whole of Freudian theory, and certainly not the abstract proposition that cultural rituals may satisfy unconscious desires.

However, before moving on, let us consider Dundes' specific hypothesis, that American football satisfies unconscious homosexual desires in the men who watch it (and participate in it). Regardless of whether you accept or reject this possibility, consider whether any other theory you have come across would attempt to answer the question of what the meaning of this ritual might be. If we went to any of the other theorists discussed in this book (or a modern representative of that theory) and asked them to explain the uniforms, terminology, and behaviors in American football, most would say that their theory is not concerned with such questions. In contrast, a psychoanalyst usually, upon reflection, has some suggestion to make about the meaning of an individual or cultural behavior. Freud's psychoanalytic theory has the largest range of applicability of any psychological theory.

I once asked a literary colleague (M. D. Faber) why he had a psychoanalytic orientation. He responded that psychoanalysis was the only theory that gave him the ability to say something about almost any literary work he read. Although other theories might *sometimes* have an insight to offer, psychoanalytic theory almost *always* had an insight to offer.

THE BASIC ASSUMPTIONS

The first basic assumption that Freud made was that all behavior is determined, and by determined he meant motivated, that is, the behavior satisfies desires. This is sometimes called the *principle of psychic determinism*. Freud, who was trained as a physician, was fully aware of the role of genetics and the physiology of the body, but in his theory he chose to focus upon mental events.

By behavior, Freud meant any observable behavior and any internal event in your mind. Your jogging is motivated by desires, as are your dreams. Furthermore, he meant *all* behavior. Your decision to take a course on personality is motivated by desires, but so is the position in which you are curled up as you read this chapter, as well as the fact that you are sucking the end of your pen or perhaps running your fingers through your hair. At this point, people tend to become defensive. They take the object from their mouth which they have been sucking and put their hands quietly in their lap. But remember, psychoanalysts do not aim to criticize. Psychoanalysts observe and analyze. They want us to know why we do the things we do, but not necessarily to stop doing them.

The second basic assumption is that almost all behaviors (observable and internal) satisfy many desires. In analyzing some behavior, we may mention only one desire that it satisfies, or perhaps two, but there are many desires involved.

Why am I a professor? Well, it pays well; I have a great deal of autonomy; I have the summer off; and I teach at most 3 days a week, which gives me time to write. I have found good friends from among my colleagues (in fact I married a colleague) and from among my students too. What else?

When I was 2 years old, I had my tonsils removed and, although my mother promised me that she would stay overnight in the hospital, they would not let her do so. After she collected me the next day, I refused to talk for 6 months and, when I did, I stuttered. She was told that stuttering was incurable, but she cured me by refusing to listen to me unless I spoke without stuttering, even though doing so "broke her heart," as she said. Demosthenes, the noted orator in ancient Greece, stuttered. Could being a professor be a compensation for my stuttering? Do I prove to myself each time I lecture that I am not a stutterer and, thereby, reassure myself?

When I was a youth, I used to daydream of being an actor. But I was too shy to act, and so I ended up as stage manager for the plays at my school. Who would I like to be? Mick Jagger—to sing and prance on the stage and have thousands of screaming fans. Well, in my class I have 35 appreciative (though hardly screaming) fans who laugh at my jokes and, sometimes, tell me what a good lecturer I am. Is this why I teach?

And so on. How many motives could I list after an exhaustive analysis of why I teach. And the same goes for your behaviors. Speculate. See how many possible desires could be motivating some behavior of yours.

The third assumption is that some of the desires motivating human behavior are unconscious. This is where many skeptical students dissent. It is difficult to convince you that you have unconscious desires because, by definition, the desires are not available to your conscious mind. They are in your unconscious because you could not tolerate knowing that you have such desires. In fact, were they suddenly to become conscious, you might have a panic attack or a psychotic breakdown. But it is possible to suggest ways in which you might discover an unconscious desire. Let me suggest two exercises here.

The next time you are are depressed ask yourself, "Could I be angry at someone? To whom have I just talked or written, thought about, dreamt about, etc.? Could I be angry at them?" Go to your bedroom by yourself and take one of the pillows. Hit it, again and again. Say "I hate you, M," where M is the name of the person you recently had in mind. Now how do you feel? If your depression was really blocked anger about which you were unaware, and if you chose the right person to project onto the pillow, then you will find that your depression has lifted and now you feel anger. Thus, your depression was due to suppressed anger.

Or, do you have a hostile teasing relationship with someone? Perhaps they tease you in a hostile fashion or you tease them? Or perhaps two of your friends tease each other in a hostile fashion. Let us say that it is you and a friend of the opposite sex who do this to each other. Now ask yourself, "Could I be sexually attracted to this person?" Often you will find that you are, or that they are attracted to you. The hostile teasing is a way of satisfying the sexual desire without becoming aware of the desire.

In each of these examples, psychoanalysis gives no guidance with what you should do with this new knowledge. If you realize that you are sexually attracted to your friend, you can continue to tease, you can suggest an affair, you can avoid them altogether, or you can find some alternative method of interacting. It does not matter which choice you make, only that it is an *informed* choice.

THE ID, EGO, AND SUPEREGO

Earlier sections described how the basic elements of psychoanalytic theory are desires (or wishes). A more neutral term would be *psychological forces*, but that is too vague for common use. Freud distinguished three *subsets of wishes*: the id, the ego, and the superego.

This is an important statement. The id, ego, and superego are not "things." They are not structures. They do not exist. They are *labels*, hypothetical constructs. Ideally they should be used only as adjectives. This is an id wish. That is a superego wish. Think of the terms *ego, id, and superego* as colors. You can have a blue shirt or a red tie, but not a blue or a red.

(Consider how much less controversy would have arisen over intelligence if the word had been used only as an adjective: e.g., "This is an intelligent response to this question or task." If it is used as a noun, many people feel instead that it is a real quantity that can be measured, for example, by an intelligence test.)

Id wishes are those that you had as an infant and child and that, typically, you were punished for and forbidden to satisfy directly or that you grew out of. Often, though not always, they are unconscious. For example, as a baby you wanted to suck at your mother's breast or at a bottle. Nowadays you do not want to do so. But the desire is still there in your unconscious.

Even if you have the desire today, it is not exactly the same as it was when you were an infant. When my son was angry once, he told me that he wanted to smash me with a cement truck, and then he ran out of the room. Today, he still gets angry at me but, as an adult, he merely refrains from calling me on the telephone or he complains about me to his friends.

Watching infants and children can often give us clues as to which desires become labeled as id desires. Or observe yourself under stress. You have been ill, but you are recovering. What foods do you eat? Probably what your mother fed you as a baby. My mother gave me soft-boiled eggs, and she cut the buttered bread into thin strips and dipped them into the egg yolk, calling them soldiers. As I recover from influenza these days, I always cook myself soft-boiled eggs, though I no longer cut the buttered bread into soldiers!

Superego desires are those we take over from important figures in our lives, mainly our parents, but also our siblings, relatives, friends, and heroes. They want us to be clean, succeed at our academic studies, join the family firm, believe in the same religion, and so on. Looking around us, we can see how well socialized we all are. We have accepted most of the desires others had for us. Even the most horrible criminals probably dress fashionably, speak the appropriate language of their culture, eat food with the proper utensils, and go to the toilet properly. Although the unsocialized part of the criminal may offend, and even horrify, us, it accounts for only a small part of their behavior.

Ego desires are the desires of the mature and rational adult. They are also compromises between the id desires and superego desires. You are angry at your father and would like to strike out at him (id desire), but you feel a little guilty for feeling anger toward him (superego desire—Honor thy mother and father). So you write him an angry letter instead or hang up on him, or perhaps you accidentally on purpose forget his birthday (ego desires)?

Traditionally psychoanalysts saw the id subset of wishes as present from birth on, with the ego subset developing after a few months and the superego subset of desires after a year or two. However, for a baby, id and ego desires are the same. It is only from an adult perspective that we label certain of our desires as id desires because they are those we had as infants and children. Furthermore, the baby can do little or nothing without the parents deciding that it is all right to do so. The baby wants food, and the parents decide that the baby ought to have food when they give the baby the bottle. So id/ego desires *and* external (later to become superego) desires both get satisfied when the baby feeds. Thus, it makes sense to assume that the desires in all three subsets of desires (the id, ego, *and* superego subsets) begin to develop at birth, though perhaps not necessarily at the same rate.

Freud described only three subsets of desires. There is nothing sacred about having three and only three, or even having these three. We should feel free to postulate additional subsets or completely different sets. For example, Chapter 6 discusses Andras Angyal's proposal of a type of desire that Freud's classification system ignores (*homonomous* desires—desires in which the individual seeks to become one with others and with the natural world). Are additional categories needed? Certainly, other theorists (such as Abraham Maslow) have categorized desires very differently from the way in which Freud classified them (see Chapter 3).

DEVELOPMENT

What are the essential features of psychological development? From a Freudian perspective there are two components. First we form derivative desires. For example, babies first drink only mother's milk; small children will accept several liquids; and adults will drink perhaps hundreds of different liquids in the course of a year. All of these desires (for cola, tea, cocktails, spring water, etc.) derive from the first, single desire one had as a baby.

Forming derivative desires gives us control. If we desire only one or two liquids, then not to have either leads to great distress and perhaps a temper tantrum. When you went to buy a cola from the cafeteria yesterday and the machine had broken, you did not cry or stamp your foot in anger! You bought coffee instead. Forming derivative desires enables us to deal with *loss*.

Remember the time when you started a hobby. Before you did so, you had at most one or two desires concerning, say, wines. But as you developed your interest, you began to desire different types of wine, to take trips to visit vineyards, to attend wine-tasting parties, to read books on wine, and perhaps to make your own wine. A whole set of desires derived from a single earlier desire.

Forming derivative desires involves *cathexis*. Cathexis is the process of learning about an object or a desire, learning to like it and appreciate it, perhaps learning to love it. We become connoisseurs of what we cathect. The baby cathects the mother's breast; we cathect our lovers. You are (I hope) cathecting psychoanalytic theory right at this moment. Learning theory can play a role here, and almost any learning theory is compatible with psychoanalytic theory.

The second way in which we develop is that we gain control over the conditions under which our desires can be gratified. As hungry babies, all we could do was cry and hope that someone fed us. As children, we could open the refrigerator and get something to eat. As adults, we can earn enough money to pay for exactly the food we want in a restaurant or we can learn to cook it the way we want. I have a friend who spent a week cooking broccoli for differing lengths of times in boiling water (measured in seconds) until he found exactly how he liked it cooked!

ANXIETY

Anxiety is a central concept in most theories of personality. How does anxiety arise in Freud's theory?

There are two sources of anxiety in Freudian theory. First, anxiety is aroused whenever desires are deprived. With some exceptions (such as extreme starvation), the greater the deprivation, the greater the anxiety. If you are hungry, cold, lonely, and feeling purposeless in life, you will also feel anxious in the Freudian sense. Some desires can not be satisfied. We have to give up the breast, bottle, and pacifier. We have to become toilet trained. We have to stop throwing food across the table. These desires become unconscious and, thereafter, are not permitted direct conscious gratification. These desires, therefore, are a major source of anxiety.

More interestingly, we become anxious whenever an unconscious desire is stimulated and is in danger of becoming conscious. We become anxious because we cannot tolerate the knowledge of this desire, knowledge in both an intellectual and an emotional sense. After all, that is why the desire is unconscious. You can use this to speculate about your own unconscious desires. Whenever you feel anxious (or perhaps embarrassed), ask yourself what unconscious desire is possibly being stimulated. Assume that each of us has every possible desire that any person has ever had. The desire is either conscious or unconscious. So which desire is being stimulated and making you anxious?

Once when I was visiting my mother as she lay in the hospital awaiting surgery the next day, I had an anxiety attack and felt I had to get some fresh air. I fled the hospital room. Later I asked myself what unconscious desire was being stimulated at that time. My mother was scared and wanting to be hugged. I could not hug her. Why? Was it an unconscious incestuous desire of the kind I had when I was 4 or 5 years old? Or was it anger welling up from resentment that had accumulated over the years? I could not decide. But I asked the question, and I speculated. An informed person is a wiser person. Perhaps next time I will not have to flee.

This double source of anxiety is the essence of Freud's theory of personality. In a later chapter, we shall call this kind of statement the *system principle*: The basic motivation for human existence is to keep our anxiety level at a minimum. To do this we have to satisfy our unconscious desires (to keep the anxiety level low) while remaining unconscious of the desires (to keep our anxiety level low).

You see the dilemma here. To keep our anxiety level low we make strange and bizarre choices that often make little sense to us. We fall in love with and marry someone who is a parent-substitute without realizing it, but then discover that something has gone wrong in the marriage. We fear open spaces even though we know rationally that we have to nothing to fear out there. We start fights with particular people without knowing why. In each case, we are satisfying an unconscious desire while remaining unconscious of what the desire really is.

A RESEARCH STUDY OF THE PSYCHOANALYTIC THEORY OF PARANOIA

Several years ago, I decided to review the research evidence relevant to a specific psychoanalytic hypothesis, and I chose the hypothesis that paranoid delusions are motivated by unconscious homosexual impulses, a hypothesis whose validity I doubted. Surprising to me, my review indicated that there was good support for the hypothesis, though the evidence was not completely consistent (Lester, 1975).

In one of the studies supporting the theory, Zamansky (1958) first developed an experimental situation in which heterosexual and homosexual men differed. He showed them pairs of slides, supposedly for the purpose of testing their accuracy in perception as to which picture was larger. Some of the pairs of pictures consisted of a picture of a man and a picture of a woman. Unknown to the subjects, hidden observers monitored the eye fixation time to each picture. Not surprisingly, the homosexual men looked at the man in each pair for a longer period of time whereas the heterosexual men looked at the woman for a longer period of time.

Zamansky then gave this task to 20 male patients at a state psychiatric hospital diagnosed with paranoid schizophrenia or paranoia and 20 male schizophrenic patients with no paranoid symptoms. Each patient judged 24 pairs of pictures, of which 9 consisted of opposite-sex pairs. The viewing time was left up to the patients.

The paranoid patients looked at the male in each pair for an average of 1.49 seconds longer than the female, whereas the non-paranoid patients looked at the female in each pair for an average of 0.70 seconds longer than the male. The difference was statistically significant at the .001 level.

However, when asked which of the pictures they preferred, the paranoid patients chose the male of each pair as equally often as did the non-paranoid patients. Thus, their preference for the male figure was unconscious and inconsistent with their conscious preference.

So, paranoid male psychiatric patients behave on this task in the same way as do homosexual men, while non-paranoid psychiatric patients behave in the same way as do heterosexual men. This study supports, therefore, Freud's hypothesis that unconscious homosexual desires are salient for schizophrenic patients with paranoid symptoms.

DEFENSE MECHANISMS

Defense mechanisms are common ways in which people solve this dilemma about anxiety. Each mechanism involves leaving the original desire unconscious, a process called *repression*, while substituting a different desire or object.

In *displacement*, which is often conscious, we change the object of the desire. We are angry at a boss, but we kick the dog, shout at the children, and slam the car door. Here we know that we are not really angry at the dog or the children or the car and that we have changed the object of our anger. In *sublimation*, the displacement is long-term and unconscious. If a child becomes angry at a parent and goes into the yard and chops down a tree, that child is displacing. If he or she becomes a logger, is that person perhaps sublimating? If a child wants to play with the messy substance in a diaper but is punished for doing so, and so plays in a mud puddle outside instead, that child is displacing. But if that child grow up to become a sculptor using clay and other moldable materials, is that perhaps sublimation?

My son wanted to play with me one day, but I was building shelves. So he went and got his plastic tool set and knocked a plastic nail into a plastic block with his plastic hammer. He *introjected* my desire. Rather than playing with me, he did what I was doing. Of course, at first, he did this right under my feet until I moved him away to the other side of the room. At least he was with me, in the same room, and doing what Daddy was doing. He got some satisfaction. (Watching him, I noticed that he cursed each time that he hit his nail. I realized that he thought that cursing was some magic mantra that had to accompany woodwork and that I must curse a lot while working!) However, if he grows up and adopts many of my desires, so that he talks like me, walks like me, votes like me, and behaves like me in many ways, then we say that he has *identified* with me, or that identification has taken place.

In *reaction formation*, the desire that appears is the opposite of the unconscious desire. Love becomes hate or hate becomes love. Think back to the hostile teasing situations I asked you to consider earlier. Sexual desire may be manifested as hostile teasing—love showing itself as hate, though in a less extreme way.

The behaviors motivated by defense mechanisms are not as satisfying as it would be to satisfy the original, now unconscious, desire. If we could just give our baby brother a good whack, we would be done for the week. But we have to play with him instead, so in the process we accidentally hurt him as we hit him, bump into him, or take his toys away. And all the while, we can justify our behavior as accidental because we were entertaining our beloved baby brother. We have to engage in this substitute behavior a lot because it is not as satisfying as a good whack would be. These substitute behaviors appear to be *driven*, that is, beyond the individual's control, and such behaviors puzzle observers because the person shows the behavior too often. We ask, "I wonder what is *really* motivating him?"

All defense mechanisms (these and others) involve cathecting the new desire and avoiding situations that might stimulate the unconscious desire—miniphobias.

PSYCHOSEXUAL STAGES

In order to describe development at the abstract level Freud made an obvious and unobjectionable proposition: the desires that are noteworthy and salient to the person and interesting to the observer change with age. It would be hard to disagree with this.

However, for personal and cultural reasons, Freud proposed a particular classification of these changing desires that outraged scholars at the time and that still outrage some people today. (Freud was seeking fame, and fame is not achieved by being reasonable. Outrageousness gets one noticed. Furthermore, as Freud lived in Europe during the Victorian era, an especially repressed time, stressing sexuality was even more likely to cause an outcry.)

Freud focused on the fact that the baby for the first year of life appears to explore the world through its mouth. After all, the baby feeds by sucking and puts almost any object it can grasp into its mouth. Freud called the stage *oral*, and this is not a bad choice of words. Erik Erikson (1968) focused on the interpersonal world of the person and drew attention to the fact that the baby learns to either trust and mistrust its caretakers during this stage and that dependency needs are salient. But the term *oral* is taken by psychoanalysts to include these aspects also.

In the second and third years of life, the baby realizes that there are babies and adults, the oppressed and oppressors. The baby begins to get some control over its muscles and so can manipulate the world a little. Power struggles now become salient. The "terrible twos" are well known to (and dreaded by) parents.

One of these power struggles concerns toilet training. The parents want the child to defecate in a toilet rather than in diapers, and to go at appropriate times, whereas the child does not always want to do so. Freud called this stage of development the *anal* stage, a poor term since it emphasizes this particular power struggle, making it appear to be the only one. Toman (1960) suggested the term *manipulatory* phase instead, but his suggestion has been ignored. Erikson (1968) called this stage *autonomy versus shame and doubt* and felt that children here develop the courage to be themselves.

From 3 to 6 years of age, the child now realizes that there are two sexes: men and women, boys and girls. They become interested in this, and they now begin to be attracted to the opposite sex parent and see the same sex parent as a rival. This is the so-called *Oedipal conflict*, named after the ancient King of Thebes who murdered his father and married his mother. The term is usually applied to both boys and girls, although the term *Electra conflict* can be used for girls. This attraction is not shown in an adult way. Children may try to get into bed with the parents, especially to snuggle in between them, thereby separating them. They may enjoy playing with either parent but have difficulty in being with both at the same time. Freud called this stage the *phallic* stage. Erikson (1968) called this stage *initiative versus guilt* and saw it as a time when children begin to practice the roles they will have as adults and learn to inhibit inappropriate behavior.

After these three stages, the child is said to enter the *latency* phase until puberty and, for psychoanalysts, little of interest happens here. Other psychologists, however, find this period to have important implications for human development.

By calling these stages *psychosexual* stages, Freud shocked people by implying that children could have sexual feelings. People thought that this meant that the sexual feelings in children had to be exactly the same as those in adults. Of course not! Erikson (1968) called these stages (along with the later ones) *psychosocial* stages, a better term. Despite the problems with the term *psychosexual*, psychoanalysts have not proposed an alternative term.

Some critics criticize stage descriptions because, they say, stages imply a rigid progression from one stage to the next and rigid transition points. Stage theories in psychology rarely imply this. It is understood that stages merge into one another and overlap, and that not everyone passes through the stages in the same sequence. All stages provide are approximate ages at which certain behaviors occur and an approximate sequence that most individuals follow.

RATE OF PSYCHOLOGICAL FUNCTIONING

The notion that the mind has an optimal rate of functioning and that this optimal rate may be different for each of us has a long history (Lester, 1986). In psychoanalytic theory the concept appears as the *rate of cathexis* (Toman, 1960). The rate of cathexis, that is, the rate with which we learn about and learn to appreciate new objects and new desires, determines how quickly we form derivative desires. If our rate of cathexis is high, we will develop more derivative desires and develop them sooner. This in turn will facilitate coping with loss since such a person will have more substitute objects and desires with which to replace the lost ones. This person will be more psychologically resilient.

Although we each have a characteristic rate of cathexis throughout our life, transient fluctuations occur from moment to moment, day to day. These are caused by deprivation of our desires. The more generally deprived we are at any particular moment, the lower our current rate of cathexis. Imagine reading this chapter to learn about psychoanalytic theory when you are tired, hungry, lonely, or rejected by your lover. The more deprived you were, the less you would cathect (learn about) this information.

Or, to take another example, imagine that you are hungry, so hungry you could eat a horse. You go to a fast-food restaurant and order two cheeseburgers. You probably will not taste the first one. You merely ingest it quickly and savagely. Ah, now you are less hungry. As you eat the second one you can begin to critique it. Is it good as you remember? Does this fast-food chain prepare them as well as the rival chain? Does this cheeseburger need extra ketchup on it? You can cathect the food better the less hungry you are.

This notion of an optimal rate of psychological functioning has been noted by other theorists. Leuba (1955), Berlyne (1960), and Hebb and Thompson (1968) gave the concept a physiological flavor and talked of an optimal level of *brain arousal*. Fiske and Maddi (1961) talked of an optimal level of *activation*. McReynolds (1956) used an information-processing analogy and talked of the rate of *perceptualization*, the rate with which we receive and assimilate percepts (or information).

Selye (1974) gave it a more folksy quality when he noted that we each have to find our optimal rate of functioning. There are racehorses and turtles, he said (and, we might add, animals with speeds in between), and each of us has to find out what type we are. Racehorses cannot go slow, and turtles cannot go fast. But if we find our own optimal level we will feel minimal stress.

Why are we curious? The notion of an optimal rate of cathexis provides an answer. Whatever our own rate of cathexis, if we stay in one environment, eventually we will cathect the objects in this environment fully. We will have learned everything about them that can be learned. What then can we cathect? We cannot cathect nothing, for then our rate of cathexis will fall below its optimal level for us. Thus, we have to go out and find new objects to explore and form derivative desires so that we will have material to cathect in order to keep our rate of cathexis what it needs to be for us. We are forced to explore and, thereby, grow.

DISTURBED BEHAVIOR

Disturbed behavior can be described in various ways using psychoanalytic theory. For example, the strength of the id, ego, and superego subsets of desires can be used to describe various disorders. Those with depressive disorders may have too strong a superego subset of desires, and those who show criminal behavior without shame, guilt, or remorse (the so-called psychopath, sociopath, or person with an antisocial personality disorder), may have too weak a superego subset. Schizophrenics may have too strong an id subset and too weak an ego subset to inhibit the direct expression of their id desires. However, such a description only raises an additional question—for example, why does this person have too strong a superego subset of desires?

The only *causal* explanation of disturbed behavior is that frustration and deprivation of desires has occurred in the first 6 years of life. This may be termed *trauma*, but what makes the events traumatic is that objects of desires are lost or that the desires are forbidden satisfaction. Some deprivation of desires is inevitable. Children have to be weaned and toilet trained and socialized in all kinds of ways. But some children experience severe trauma.

What makes a trauma severe? Much depends on the child's subjective experience. For an infant, there may be little difference between being hit by an abusive parent and having a needle injection by a caring physician. Furthermore, what may seem very traumatic to us (such as physical abuse) often does not result in as severe a psychiatric disorder as some ways of talking to a child (which may seriously damage self-esteem).

There are two general rules for how severe the later disturbed behavior will be.

1. The earlier in life the trauma occurs, the more severe the later psychiatric disorder. Loss of a mother at age 2 is more traumatic than loss of her at the age of 5.
2. The more severe the loss involved, the more severe the later psychiatric disorder. Loss of a mother at age 2 is probably more traumatic than loss of a father, at least in the traditional family.

However, the theory is typically not as good at *predicting* later behavior from an examination of the trauma suffered by children as *explaining* the later behavior after the event. Particular traumatic incidents do not result in the same adult behaviors (or symptoms) for everyone later in adulthood. The incident interacts with other life experiences and with the individual's mind to

THE CASE OF AN EXHIBITIONIST

What kind of understanding does a psychoanalyst develop about a client? An example is provided by McCawley (1965) who worked with a theological student who was having marital problems with his wife and who exposed himself to young boys and girls. At the time of the offense, his wife was critical of his ambitions, belittled him, and often interrupted their love-making, refusing to resume it. He was also about to be given increased responsibility at the seminary. After his arrest for exhibitionism, he had to leave the seminary to become a psychiatric inpatient for a while, after which his wife divorced him.

He eventually remarried, and his second wife was sexually compatible with him. His father offered him some money to start a small business but then began to criticize him for the way he was running the business. As the stress grew, the man again exposed himself to a young girl and was arrested.

The man's father was a hard-working business man who was often away from home while his children were growing up, and who had always been hostile to his son and belittled him. The mother was hostile to all of her children. Thus, the young man had never received much affection from his parents. McCawley guessed that he had failed to model himself on (identify with) either of them. He had only one close friendship as a child, another boy at school, and the two of them used to expose themselves to each other occasionally. McCawley hypothesized that the young man regressed to this stage of his development when he was under stress.

At the time of the first episode of exhibitionism, the young man was overwhelmed by feelings of inferiority and sexual inadequacy. At the time of the second episode, he was feeling inadequate about his business acumen. On each occasion he was angry, at his first wife and then at his father. However, in psychotherapy, it took many sessions before he was able to feel and express this anger. He eventually realized that each episode of exhibitionism removed him from stressful situations, first his difficult marriage and responsibility at the seminary, and then from business pressures.

The anger he felt toward his first wife and toward his father was made stronger by the intense unconscious anger he had felt as a child toward his rejecting mother and father. This anger was unconscious, most likely because his parents punished him for expressing the anger toward them, as many parents do. The relationship with his first wife recapitulated his relationship with his mother, and so was especially stressful for him. The business venture with his father recapitulated his early relationship with his father. The regression to an early pattern of behavior symbolizes the wish to be a child again and to avoid adult responsibilities.

If this analysis is valid, once the client is aware of the psychodynamics behind his behavior, he can devise more acceptable ways of expressing his feelings toward the people at whom he is angry, or perhaps find ways of avoiding the situations that arouse his anger. He can also find ways of dealing with stress other than by exhibitionism.

produce a unique pattern of reactions which is difficult to predict. However, in retrospect the pattern of reactions "makes sense."

All intrapsychic theories agree that early trauma is the only causal factor in the development of disturbed behavior. The theories differ, however, in the kind of trauma on which they focus.

PSYCHOTHERAPY

As mentioned earlier in this chapter, the goal of psychoanalysis as a psychotherapeutic strategy is to give clients insight into the motivations that are

IS FREUD DEAD?

Every few years the question is asked whether Freudian theory is outdated or, put more colorfully, "dead"? Let us look at the reasons that Gray (1993), one recent writer on this topic, advanced supporting the supposition that Freudian theory has outlived its usefullness, and some refutations of his points

1. Gray noted the proliferation of accusations of sexual abuse in childhoods of patients who have been guided by psychotherapists in recalling memories that have been presumably repressed for many years. Some of these memories have turned out to be false, that is, the abuse did not happen. Thus, Freud's theory is being misused by some psychotherapists.

    The misuse of a theory by psychotherapists who base their clinical practice on the theory does not invalidate the theory. For example, several leading physiological researchers have been accused in recent years of scientific fraud. A Nobel Prize–winner, David Baltimore, apparently allowed himself to be co-author of a paper, the data of which may have been fraudulent, and he resisted efforts to investigate the possible fraud. This does not invalidate physiological research in general or the theories behind it.

2. Gray cited the recent success of medications in treating psychiatric disorders. He felt that this argues against the validity of Freudian theory.

    The study of the mind has changed in theoretical orientation, swinging from an emphasis on the role of life experiences in the 1960s to an emphasis now on the role of physiology. The 1990s in particular have witnessed a growth in the media reporting of research demonstrating the role of genetic and physiological factors on human behavior. This does not mean that there is no role for psychological factors. For example, let us assume, as is widely believed these days, that the neurotransmitter serotonin is found to be the basis for depression and suicidal behavior (Lester, 1988). Can that neurotransmitter explain why American poet Sylvia Plath committed suicide with gas from a kitchen stove at age 30, whereas English writer Virginia Woolf drowned herself at the age of 59 (Lester, 1990a). (Interestingly, both writers lost a parent during their childhoods, an experiential factor relevant to their later depressions and life courses).

3. Modern health care plans do not pay for psychoanalysis. Many health insurance plans never did pay for intensive psychotherapy, and plans that did pay always had limits that would have excluded psychoanalysis.

behind the choices they make. This particular approach to psychotherapy takes a great deal of time, perhaps three 1-hour sessions a week for 5 to 10 years. The more difficult it is for a client to get in touch with their unconscious desires, the longer the psychotherapy will take.

Psychoanalysts use three major techniques for achieving this insight: *free association, transference,* and *interpretation.*

Free Association

In free association, clients say whatever comes into their minds when they bring up an issue. Typically these associations are of events earlier in their life. Perhaps our client remembers a dream from the previous night. She tells it and then she remembers an incident that actually happened the previous day, which then reminds her of something that happened when she was a child, which then reminds her . . . and so on. As the web of associations develops, not just to today's stimulus, but to those of last week and of next week, the

Psychoanalysis has always been a psychotherapy for the rich. Furthermore, psycho-analysis as a system of psychotherapy is not the same as psychoanalysis as a theory of the mind, and problems with the one are not always pertinent to the other.

4. Several criticisms have appeared detailing errors and "fudged" data in psychoanalysis. The first three points raised by Gray are irrelevant to the usefulness and the validity of psychoanalytic theory; this point may have more truth. Let us look at it in detail.

First, Gray tells us that the split between Freud and one of his early supporters, Carl Jung, was in part a result of Freud's suspicion that Jung was having an affair with one of his clients, while Jung suspected that Freud was involved with his sister-in-law. Gray asks us, "Was this any way to found an objective science?" The personal lives of scholars have no relevance to the usefulness or validity of their theories.

Second, Gray tells us that other scholars have found alternative psychodynamic mechanisms to explain the symptoms of one of Freud's clients and, related to this, Freud may have tried to fit patients into his preconceived opinions about them. Freud's skill as a psychotherapist again has no relevance to the validity of his theory of personality.

Finally, Gray refers to scholars who argue that Freud did not "prove" any of his assertions. To this, Freud would have to plead guilty. It would be difficult to formulate a psychoanalytic theory of the mind in a way that would permit testing of predictions derived from the theory so that they could be confirmed or refuted. As stated in Chapter 4, psychoanalytic theory is a "loose" theory, that is a theory that does not lead to clear, unambiguous predictions. However, that criticism may be true of many of the theories presented in this volume. Although some predictions from the theories can formulated precisely and tested empirically, many of the basic concepts concern hypothetical con-structs, the existence of which cannot be confirmed.

So, is Freud dead? I think not. The criticisms advanced by Gray are largely irrelevant to the validity or the usefulness of theory, except for the failure of the theory to conform to the structure of theories formulated in the natural sciences, but this characteristic may be what allows it to explain the diversity of human behavior.

psychoanalyst and the client begin to see the connections between early events and later events and the unconscious desires which affect today's choices.

Transference

Psychoanalysts prefer to remain out of sight of the client and to say very little, especially at first. In this way, the client begins to transfer emotions and desires felt toward others (such as a parent or a spouse) onto the psychoanalyst. The client treats the psychoanalyst as if she were his parent, for example. In this way, the client and psychoanalyst can see how the client in fact feels toward his mother. It brings the "outside world" into the psychotherapeutic situation a little.

Interpretation

The psychoanalyst also explains to the client why he behaves the way he does and what his unconscious desires might be. The best interpretations are those reached by the client himself for then he is ready to accept them. So psychoanalysts try to lead their clients into insight slowly so that the insights come from the clients themselves. This is why psychoanalysis takes such a long time.

The goal, then, is insight—not changing behavior and certainly not making one happy. However, once clients have insight into the motives behind their behavior, it will be difficult for them to behave in exactly the same way again. If, for example, you realize that you are teasing a colleague because of sexual attraction, it will be difficult to act in the same way now that you know this.

DISCUSSION

I have tried in this nontraditional presentation of Freud's theory of psycho-analysis to use as little psychoanalytic jargon as possible and to present the theory in as rational a way as possible. The theory has several implications.

First, as in all intrapsychic theories, the locus for the causal factors of human behavior lies in the mind. Even though Freud was well aware of the influences of other people in our lives, it is the way in which we perceive their actions that is crucial. For example, which of their desires do we introject and which, therefore, get added to our superego subset of desires?

Second, it is an historical approach. The important events in our lives occur in the first 6 years of life. Parents tend to reject this idea since it places such a great a burden on them and, to be honest, at times as I interacted with my infant son, I too found myself anxious over the implications of what I was doing and saying to him.

Third, it is a *loose* theory (a term defined in Chapter 4, which presents George Kelly's theory of personal constructs), that is, it does not lead to clear unambiguous predictions. The theory permits us to explain any outcome *once we know what happened*. From a formal scientific point of view, this is a serious drawback. However, human behavior is so complex that a tight theory, which makes clear and unambiguous predictions and is capable of refutation, would be refuted most of the time. Let me give you an example.

When I was a graduate student, I conducted some research on rats as a hobby. I taught one group of rats to turn left in a simple maze in order to obtain food. They received four trials a day. Simple learning theory predicted that rewarding the rats on the left should make them turn left more and more often until they never made errors (by turning right). In general this was correct. But I had deviant rats.

One rat, for example, on the first trial of each day would anchor her two back feet just outside the place on the right arm of the maze where the guillotine door would have closed behind her had she placed all four feet in the arm. She would then stretch forward cautiously, and her whiskers would search for indications that I had switched the location of the food on her. Then she would carefully back up, keeping her back two feet still outside the arm, and then she would enter the left arm for food. On the next three trials that day, she would turn left without hesitation. Her behavior was understandable, but it did not follow the laws of simple learning theory.

If rats do not follow these simple laws, then it is no wonder that humans do not either. Human behavior is much too complex to be explained on the basis of a limited number of rigid principles, laws, or rules. There will always be exceptions to such rigid rules, and exceptions here do *not* "prove the rule."

I like to think of psychoanalytic theory as similar to providing an artist with oil paints, brushes, and canvases. These tools limit what can be produced to some extent. But a walk around any major art museum will quickly illustrate the diversity of paintings that can be produced even with these limitations, i.e., hundreds of paintings, none like any other.

Freud's psychoanalytic theory provides particular assumptions and terms that limit our ability to describe human experience to some extent. But we are still able to create millions of different minds, none like any other. No other theory of personality has the power to capture the uniqueness of each of our individual experiences and personalities.

3

Modifications to Freudian Ideas

Several personality theorists have suggested modifications to Freudian ideas, and this chapter reviews some of these suggestions. The first major modification was suggested by Carl Jung whose view of the unconscious was quite different from Freud's.

CARL JUNG'S CONCEPT OF THE UNCONSCIOUS

Freud saw the unconscious as mainly comprised of desires that were prominent in infancy and childhood, desires for which the child was punished and desires that the child was supposed to outgrow, that is, id wishes. Thus, the Freudian unconscious has a somewhat negative connotation, as it is the repository of infantile desires.

Carl Jung agreed with Freud that the mind contained a set of conscious contents and a set of unconscious contents similar to the Freudian unconscious, which Jung called the *personal unconscious* (Jung, 1971). However, Jung saw these two components of the mind as relatively minor. Jung proposed that there was also a part of the the mind that was called the *collective unconscious*. The contents of this part of the mind were, according to Jung, common to all humans, a set of themes inherited and, therefore, very similar to the collective unconscious of humans thousands of years ago. These themes contained in the collective unconscious, called *archetypes* by Jung, are fundamental symbolic patterns. Because these themes are shared by all humans, past and present, and are therefore unaffected by the language of any particular culture, they must be symbolized in nonverbal images.

Jung and his followers have sought to identify and describe archetypes. To do this, they look for themes in a variety of cultures, in art and literature, in our dreams and in the psychotic delusions and hallucinations of patients.

For example, the hero archetype usually contains the hero's miraculous yet humble birth. Early in his life, he shows superhuman strength (physical or spiritual), and sometimes has a tutor who helps him. There is a rapid rise to power and fame as he battles the forces of evil. The hero falls from power either because of his pride or because of a betrayal, and he dies in a heroic sacrifice. Examples of heroes and their "tutors" abound: Achilles and Cheiron, Perseus and Athena, Theseus and Poseidon, King Arthur and Merlin, Jesus and the Lord, and Superman and his father. This theme is so common, however, that communication of the theme from one culture to another cannot be ruled out as an explanation for its frequent occurrence.

Jung (1971) gave a more convincing example. He recalled an encounter with a paranoid schizophrenic in the psychiatric hospital in which he worked who told Jung to look at the sun. If he did so, he would see the sun's penis. If Jung were to move his head from side to side, the sun's penis would also move, and that was the origin of the wind.

Though he had read widely in philosophy, anthropology, archeology, religion, and history, Jung had, at that time never come across such an idea. However, 4 years later, he was reading about the Mithraic cult, a religion that spread from ancient Persia to Asia Minor and thence to the Roman Empire in the first century AD. One of the visions in the ancient text explained the origin of the wind by proposing that a tube hangs down from the sun from which the wind emerges. Jung immediately recalled the hallucination of the patient in his hospital several years previously. He then thought about this image more extensively and realized that the Holy Ghost, which is described as a "mighty rushing wind," was sometimes depicted in medieval paintings as impregnating the Virgin Mary through a tube from the heavens that reached down under her robe. This theme and image is sufficiently uncommon that it is much more difficult to account for its occurrence by proposing cultural transmission. Jung assured himself that his psychiatric patient could not have read the volume on the Mithraic cult and was not acquainted with medieval painting.

Most academic psychologists have rejected the idea of the collective unconscious, preferring to see the global similarity of themes as a result of the diffusion over time from one culture to another as peoples migrated around the world. Progoff (1973), however, suggested a method by which archetypes could be inherited that might make it more acceptable to scholars. He argued that the archetype itself was not inherited. Rather, we inherit the capacity to generate archetypes similar to those generated by others because we share similar structures in our psyches.

An example might be castration anxiety in males. Men do not inherit castration anxiety. They inherit genes for an anatomical structure (a penis), which has the possibility of being cut off. Hence, they will inevitably develop castration anxiety.

Noam Chomsky's proposal of a universal linguistic grammar, the basis for which is inherited in the structure of the mind, is analogous. Chomsky (1975) argued that people could not possibly produce the complex linguistic utterances they make, even as children, simply by modeling their linguistic behavior on the utterances made by others. He suggested that humans inherit the capacity to generate a universal grammar. Once they hear particular examples of their native language, the universal grammar generated within their own minds deciphers the particular grammatical rules of their particular language and enables them to generate sentences that they have never heard before (see also Pinker, 1994; Rosenberg, 1993). Academic psychologists found Chomsky's proposal provocative, and they did not dismiss it out of hand. Progoff modified Jung's notion of the collective unconscious to make it analogous to Chomsky's notion of a universal grammar, hoping thereby to make Jung's ideas more acceptable.

Jung's concept of the unconscious changes it from a repository of desires that we would find unacceptable were we aware of them to a source of creative ideas. Conscious awareness of the Freudian unconscious would lead to massive anxiety; conscious awareness of the Jungian unconscious would lead to psychological growth. The difference between the concepts can be illustrated by Freud's and Jung's views about dreams. For Freud, dreams are ways of satisfying unacceptable unconscious desires through fantasy. They are bizarre because distortion of the images is necessary so that we do not become conscious of what dreams are *really* about. In contrast, for Jung, the dream may be difficult to interpret, not because it is distorted, but because the collective unconscious uses symbols to express the ideas. The problem is not of uncovering the hidden meaning of the dream, but rather one of translating the symbolic language of dreams into the conscious symbols we are accustomed to use, namely, language.

O. HOBART MOWRER

Mowrer (1964, 1966) began his academic career by focusing on learning theory, but later in his life he proposed a theory of psychopathology and therapy. His ideas have implications for the psychoanalytic theory of personality.

For Freud, anxiety was aroused when wishes came into conflict. Freud suggested that neurotic anxiety resulted from a conflict between ego wishes and id wishes and that moral anxiety (guilt) resulted from a conflict between ego or id wishes with superego wishes. Much of human behavior was an attempt to deal with this anxiety.

Mowrer saw things somewhat differently. First of all, the crucial source of anxiety for Mowrer was moral anxiety (guilt). Second, rather than guilt resulting from a conflict between superego wishes and other wishes, guilt for Mowrer was a result of actual misdeeds, or sins. People misbehave and as a result feel guilt. Psychopathology is a result of the person trying to repress this guilt.

The healthy person acknowledges the guilt, confesses the misdeeds to an appropriate person, and makes some kind of atonement for the misdeeds. In other words, the person must confess and do penance. This type of therapeutic process is quite common, being found (though phrased in different terms) in such systems as Alcoholics Anonymous, Synanon, reality therapy, group therapy, network therapy, and the healing practices of many primitive societies.

Repression of guilt leads to several consequences. When you repress your guilt, you are no longer conscious of your superego wishes. Thus, you become cut off from society's values. As a result, you tend to withdraw from and feel alienated from others because you no longer consciously share their values.

Second, since you repress your guilt, you are more likely to commit more misdeeds. Thus, you sin again, thereby compounding the problem.

Mowrer's position can be contrasted sharply with Freud's. For Freud, the "ego" has repressed the "id" and has been taken over by the "superego." For Mowrer, the "ego" has repressed the "superego" and been taken over by the "id."

For Freud, the neurotic's superego wishes are too strong, too powerful, too punishing. The neurotic is unable to express his id impulses even in a diluted or indirect fashion, because his superego wishes are too demanding. For Mowrer, the neurotic has learned the values of his society but, rather than accepting them, he has repressed them. For Freud the neurotic is oversocialized; for Mowrer he is undersocialized. Thus, Mowrer sees psychoanalysis as a danger-ous technique because it makes the neurotic even less socialized and turns him into an antisocial person. Mowrer saw his theory as explaining the many mixed types of neurotics and psychopaths; in his view, they are similar because they are undersocialized. In Freudian theory they are very different; the first is undersocialized whereas the latter is oversocialized. Incidentally, Mowrer ap-plied his theory both to neuroses and to psychoses.

Mowrer chose a religious metaphor on purpose. He wanted to emphasize the fact that people must be held responsible for their behavior. This emphasis, however, has led to his views as being seen as reactionary. London (1964) noted that no theory since Freud's had been subjected to such voluble and vituper-ative criticism.

Despite this reaction to the theory, it is but a modification, indeed a minor modification, of Freudian theory. It a mere shuffling around of a few concepts. The way in which the theory is phrased has aroused the strong reaction. Perhaps this points to the necessity for proposing theories of personality in neutral terms. The words chosen obviously have important implications, but the theories should stand or fall despite their implications. The implications distort the theory.

Finally, despite Mowrer's neglect by the majority of psychologists, his views on therapy are congruent with those of many other psychotherapists. Again, his choice of terms has served to isolate him from others, even though their views are compatible. Just as the nature of Freud's theory was in part a product of the repressive Victorian era, the nature of Mowrer's theory was in part a product of the laissez-faire 1960s. In Victorian times, Freud's theory implied that people could tolerate greater awareness and greater satisfaction of their id desires. In the 1960s, Mowrer's theory implied that we should control our behavior and be more concerned with whether it is consistent with our moral standards.

THE MAJOR NEEDS

Freud classified our desires primarily based upon the source (id, ego, or superego desires) and upon the infantile desires from which they derived (oral,

A RESEARCH STUDY ON MOWRER'S THEORY

Mowrer predicted that both neurotics and psychopathic individuals would be character-ized by having too weak a superego subset of desires, that is, they are not as well socialized as normal, psychologically healthy people. Peterson (1967) tested this using mildly disturbed subjects.

Peterson had the teachers in a junior high school rate every one of the 313 boys and 367 girls for the presence or absence of 58 specific problems. Of this group, 64 boys and 118 girls had no problems checked. Twenty boys and 12 girls had at least four conduct problems checked, and at least 80% of the problems checked were conduct problems. Twenty-three boys and 32 girls had at least four personality problems checked, and at least 80% of the problems checked were personality problems. These three groups constituted respectively the normal, mildly psychopathic and mildly neurotic groups.

Peterson measured how well each child was socialized by giving them the Socialization Scale of the California Psychological Inventory (Gough, 1960). For all the boys and girls in the school, the association between the number of conduct problems checked was negatively associated with the socialization score, as was the number of personality problems checked (Table 3.1).

Table 3.1 Gender differences in correlations between problems and socialixation

	Boys	Girls
Number of conduct problems	− 0.22	− 0.23
Number of personality problems	− 0.14	− 0.23

Table 3.2 gives the mean socialization scores (with standard deviations in parentheses) for the three small subgroups.

Table 3.2 Gender differences in problems

	Boys	Girls
No problems	41.8(6.2)	43.3(5.7)
Personality problems	37.6(7.7)	38.2(7.4)
Conduct problems	36.8(5.7)	35.8(7.7)

The normal children were significantly more socialized than the children with person-ality problems and those with conduct problems. Although these two latter groups did not differ significantly, the children with conduct problems did have lower average socialization scores than the children with personality problems as predicted by Mowrer.

Thus, Peterson's results confirmed Mowrer's hypothesis that people with neurotic traits are less well-socialized than normal people.

anal, and phallic). Although other personality theorists have accepted the importance of desires, they have proposed different classifications of them.

Murray's Classification of Needs

Henry Murray (1938, 1959) listed and devised ways of measuring some fundamental needs of humans. He proposed classifications of needs into vis-cerogenic (physiological) and psychogenic (psychological) needs and compiled lists of the needs in each category. The viscerogenic needs (12 in all) were classified as to whether they resulted from lacks (the body needs air, water, and food), distensions (bloating from internal pressures, such as that which occurs when one's bladder is full), or harms (such as avoiding pain) and as to whether they were positive (*adient*—eliciting approach) or negative (*abient*—eliciting avoidance). The 28 psychogenic (or secondary) needs were classified as to whether they were negative (abient) or positive (adient if the person approaches a liked object and *contrient* if the person approaches a disliked object). Needs often come into conflict, and Murray noted briefly that this is the cause of most neurotic disorders.

In considering the environment (which Murray also took to include the physiological processes of the body), Murray defined two terms. First, an object that evokes a need is said to have *cathexis* or to be *cathected*. (The term is used, therefore, differently from Freud's psychoanalytic theory.) Objects that evoke positive adient needs are said to have positive cathexis and those that evoke positive contrient needs or negative abient needs are said to have negative cathexis.

In addition, Murray classified environmental events in terms of the kinds of benefits and harms they provided. Directional tendencies in the environment he termed *press*. (Neutral environmental events are inert.) The press of an object is what it can do to the person or for the person. The cathexis of an object is what it can make the person do. The *alpha press* is the press that actually exists; the *beta press* is the person's interpretation of the environmental event. Murray proposed a classification of press to accompany his classification of needs. The beta press together with the internal processes of the person constitute the *field* (Murray and Kluckhohn, 1953).

Murray did not have any theoretical basis for his classification of needs. Rather he simply listed all the needs he could think of and grouped them as best he could.

Maslow's Hierarchy of Needs

Abraham Maslow, one of the founders of humanistic psychology, also focused on desires. Maslow felt that the study of motivation should be the study of the ultimate goals or desires of people, conscious and unconscious. Like Freud, Maslow saw any behavior as multiply motivated, that is, as a means of expressing several desires. Furthermore, he felt that people were not very different from one another in their fundamental desires.

In studying desires, Maslow (1970) did not try to list each and every specific desire. He preferred to study them in relation to one another and in general terms. Maslow classified the fundamental human desires in a sequence: physiological needs, safety needs, belongingness and love needs, esteem needs, and needs for self-actualization. (Maslow (1963) noted that he had omitted the curiosity need, because he was unsure where to place it. Thus, curiosity is usually omitted from the hierarchy.) These needs are listed in order of potency. If physiological needs are deprived, their satisfaction becomes the major goal of the person. Once physiological needs are satisfied, then safety needs become

A RESEARCH STUDY ON MASLOW'S NEEDS

Maslow proposed that psychological disturbance would be greater the more an individual's basic needs were deprived. I devised a simple self-report inventory to measure the level of deprivation of the five basic needs described by Maslow: physiological (e.g., "I never have trouble getting to sleep at night"), safety and security (e.g., "I would not walk alone in my neighborhood at night"), belonging (e.g., "I feel somewhat socially isolated"), esteem (e.g., "I feel that I am a worthy person"), and self-actualization (e.g., "I feel I am living up to my potential"). The complete inventory can be found in Lester (1990b).

The inventory was given to 42 college students along with the Eysenck Personality Inventory (Eysenck, Eysenck, & Barrett, 1985), which measures extroversion, neuroticism, and psychoticism. Table 3.3 gives the matrix of Pearson correlations.

Table 3.3

Satisfaction of needs	Extroversion	Neuroticism	Psychoticism
Physiological	0.17	-0.62^*	-0.06
Safety	0.23	-0.62^*	0.11
Belonging	0.45^*	-0.43^*	-0.30^*
Esteem	0.49^*	-0.39^*	-0.11
Self-actualization	0.40^*	-0.39^*	-0.19

* Statistically significant at the 5% level or better.

The more each basic need was satisfied, the lower the students' neuroticism scores, as predicted. However, satisfaction of the basic needs was not consistently associated with psychoticism, whereas a negative association was predicted. No prediction was made about the association between the satisfaction of basic needs and extroversion, but the associations were positive for the higher needs, that is, the more extroverted students reported more satisfaction of the higher needs (belonging, esteem and self-actualization).

This study, therefore, provided some support for Maslow's theory of needs.

the person's central purpose and so on. In addition, needs appear roughly in that sequence as the infant matures and develops into an adult, as animals evolved from amoeba to humans, and as human civilization advanced. Maslow described this hierarchy as one of *relative prepotency*. Higher needs are less imperative for sheer survival, and their gratification can be postponed for longer periods of time. Maslow saw all needs in the hierarchy in some sense and to some degree as constitutionally based and hereditary, or *instinctoid*.

Each of us may be classified as to how satisfied each of our fundamental needs is at any point in our life. For example, perhaps we are satisfied 85% in our physiological needs, 70% in our safety needs, 50% in our love needs, 40% in our esteem needs, and 10% in our self-actualization needs.

Our conscious desires are symptoms or surface indicators of the more basic needs. As with Freudian psychoanalytic theory, psychopathology for Maslow is a result of frustration of needs. The more fundamentally important the need that is frustrated, more severe the psychopathology. In addition, the greater the satisfaction of needs higher in the hierarchy of relative prepotency, the psychologically healthier the person is. Maslow also suggested that psychopathology may be unitary, that is, the separate so-called psychiatric syndromes

CAN EVERYONE BECOME SELF-ACTUALIZED?

For Abraham Maslow, self-actualization was the highest need in the hierarchy, and "self-actualized" was his term for psychologically healthy people, those who had been to able to satisfy lower needs in the hierarchy so that they been able to actualize their potential and reach a position of psychological health. Can everyone achieve this, given the right environmental circumstances and life experiences?

Some brief paragraphs in his writings indicate that Maslow was far from sure that the answer was yes. In his classic work, *Toward a Psychology of Being*, Maslow (1968) wrote, "But more recently we have been learning, especially from physically and mentally sick people, that there are good choosers and bad choosers" (pp. 150–151). He continued

Chickens allowed to choose their own diet vary widely in their ability to choose what is good for them. The good choosers become stronger, large, more dominant than the poor choosers. . . . If then the diet of the good choosers is forced upon the poor choosers, it is found that they now get stronger, bigger, healthier and more dominant . . . although never reaching the level of the good choosers. (p. 151)

Maslow felt that the poor choosers, given the best environmental circumstances, could not achieve the level of health of the poor choosers. Indeed, when I was his teaching assistant, Maslow wanted me to conduct research on animals to verify his idea. Did the same apply to humans? "Furthermore, any ethical code will have to deal with the fact of constitutional differences not only in chickens and rats but also in men" (p. 151). A little later he wrote, "it looks to me as if most people (perhaps all) tend toward self-actualization, and as if, in principle at least, most people are capable of self-actualization" (p. 158).

These extracts indicate some uncertainty. Most, but not all, people can become self-actualized, and the reason that not all can become psychologically healthy is not a result of their circumstances or life experiences, which can accomplish only so much. "The culture is sun and food and water: it is not the seed" (p. 161). What then is determined by the seed, that is, the genetic inheritance? Maslow never clarified this completely. But I felt, in my discussions with him, especially about those chickens who were poor choosers and never could be as healthy as the good choosers, that the potential to be psychologically healthy, in his view, in part inherited.

may be simply superficial and idiosyncratic reactions to a deeper, basic psychiatric illness.

Maslow advocated the study of psychologically healthy people as an important task to complement the study of psychologically disturbed people. He suggested that the motivational life of psychologically healthy (or self-actualized) people was qualitatively different from that of other people. He saw self-actualized people as more motivated by what he called growth needs, whereas others were motivated by deficiency needs. However, although he gave clinical descriptions of self-actualized people, he did not propose a *formal theory* of personality based on them.

Maslow saw motivation as a universal characteristic of practically every state of the personality. Yet he sometimes asserted that not all behavior is motivated by these fundamental needs. He saw expressive behavior, for example, as having no purpose and many somatic symptoms as having no goal or function and no motivation (either conscious or unconscious).

In summary, Maslow's classification of needs has a phylogenetic, ontogenetic, and primary basis, and so has theoretical implications. Furthermore,

Maslow followed Freud in proposing that deprivation of desires leads to later disturbed behavior.

Henri Laborit

A French scholar, Henri Laborit (1988), has suggested that Freud was wrong in his emphasis on sexual and aggressive desires as the most salient in human behavior. Laborit felt that desire for power and domination over others was the most central desire in explaining human behavior.(The French film, *Mon Oncle d'Amerique*, directed by Alain Resnais and released in the United States in 1980 by New World, presented Laborit's views using an entertaining story, interspersed with brief lectures by Laborit.) The idea that the desire for power is important for understanding human behavior may be found also in the writings of Laing (1967) and Haley (1971), as well as in feminist views on the rape and murder of women by men as the result of the eroticization of power (Caputi, 1987).

Existential Psychotherapists

Existential psychotherapists disagree with Freud's view of the unconscious. They argue that childhood concerns, particularly centered around sexuality and aggressiveness, are not an important source of anxiety. Instead they propose that existential concerns lead to anxiety and, thence, psychological disturbance. Yalom (1980) has described four major existential concerns.

1. The inevitable fact that we are, each of us, going to die, causes a great deal of anxiety but, only if we recognize and accept our mortality, can we live authentically.
2. Anxiety is aroused by the freedom we have. This freedom has two components. First, we are responsible for our actions and failures to act. Most important, we are responsible for deciding what things are significant in our lives. Nothing is important until we designate it so. Responsibility leads to guilt over our transgressions against ourselves. What have we made of ourselves? Have we realized our potential?

   Second, we have freedom insofar as we have *will*. Will is the trigger of effort and action. Because will has its limits (for example, we can will going to bed, but we cannot will sleep), patients in psychotherapy often deny that they have will.
3. The fact that we are alone is a third source of anxiety. We are not interpersonally alone, but we die alone and we alone are responsible for our actions. We need to belong, to be a part of although we are apart from. Only when we confront our isolation and aloneness can we relate to others intimately and meaningfully.
4. We often wonder what the meaning of life might be, both in general (i.e., cosmically) and specifically for us. Though some existentialists see life as meaningless, others suggest that we could not possibly understand the meaning of life while we are part of it. One cannot perceive a pattern if

one is part of the pattern—only when one steps back from the pattern. Thus, to perceive the meaning of life, we must no longer be part of life.

Despite this, Victor Frankl (1963), whose version of existential psychotherapy is called *logotherapy*, noted that we need to feel that there is a meaning in our lives, and we have to discover our own meaning—by doing some altruistic action, by dedicating ourselves to a cause, by creating, by pursuing hedonism, by self-actualization, or by changing our attitude toward our own suffering. One of the goals of logotherapy is to help clients find a meaning for their lives.

THE PSYCHOSEXUAL STAGES

Several theorists have proposed alternatives to Freud's psychosexual stages. The most well-known of these is that proposed by Erik Erikson (1950). Erikson focused on the task of establishing and maintaining a sense of identity, and he described eight stages through which a person goes, each of which involves a crisis in personality development.

1. *Infancy* In the first year of life, babies are dependent upon their caretakers, especially their mother, for the satisfaction of their desires. If their mother satisfies the baby's desires appropriately, then the baby will develop a sense of basic trust; on the other hand, if the mother frustrates the baby's desires, then the baby will develop a sense of basic mistrust. The resolution of this stage sets up a pattern for the individual's life, determining whether the person will trust others or not.
2. *Toddler Stage* As the child enters what Freud called the anal stage, when power struggles become a central feature of the child's relationship with its parents, Erikson saw the basic conflict as between autonomy as opposed to shame and doubt. If the parents permit the child to win some struggles and to lose others gracefully, then the child will come to feel independent and self-confident. If the child is not permitted to develop a sense of mastery and influence, then the child will develop feelings of shame and doubt.
3. *Early Childhood* Freud's phallic stage was seen by Erikson as crucial for the child's sense of initiative, the development of ambition and purpose in life, rather than a sense of guilt and resignation.
4. *Later Stages* Erikson then described five more stages and their conflicts for the later stages of life: stage 4, elementary school age, in which the conflict is between industry (a sense of ambition and purpose) and a sense of inferiority; stage 5, adolescence, in which the conflict is between identity (who am I?) and role confusion; stage 6, young adulthood, in which the conflict is between intimacy and isolation; stage 7, adulthood in which the conflict is between generativity (a concern for the next generation) and stagnation; and stage 8, old age, in which the conflict is between ego integrity and despair.

A STUDY USING LOEVINGER'S STAGES

Borst and Noam (1993) studied 139 girls aged 13 to 16 who were admitted as psychiatric inpatients. They used a test devised by Jane Loevinger to assess at which stage the girls were in their psychological development—preconformist or conformist. The girls were also classified as to whether they had attempted suicide prior to admission or not. Girls who reported serious suicidal ideation, but no suicide attempt, were excluded from the sample.

Preconformist people possess less mature ego-functioning and are focused on gratification of their own needs. They are egocentric and impulsive, feel helpless, and tend to depend upon and exploit others. Conformist people are much more aware of the expectations of others and have some self-awareness. Their interpersonal relationships are concerned with being accepted by others.

Among the psychological tests given to these girls was a measure of symptoms of distress that classified them as internalizing (such as, complains of loneliness, cries a great deal, and tries to be perfect) versus externalizing (such as, argues a great deal and destroys things). Table 3.4 shows how the four groups of girls differed in their symptoms.

Table 3.4 Mean symptom scores for suicidal and nonsuicidal girls

	Internal symptoms	External symptoms
Nonsuicidal/preconformist	55.8	64.3
Suicidal preconformist	64.0	67.1
Nonsuicidal/conformist	53.0	58.5
Suicidal/conformist	62.7	58.9

Suicidal girls had higher scores for internalizing symptoms than the nonsuicidal girls, but did not differ in their scores for externalizing symptoms. In contrast, the developmental level (preconformist versus conformist) was associated with the scores for externalizing symptoms but not for internalizing symptoms.

Based on this psychological test and others that they administered to the girls, Borst and Noam concluded that preconformist suicidal girls are angry and action-oriented, have a limited capacity for self-reflection, and direct their aggression toward others as well as themselves. Borst and Naom called the suicidal preconformist girls the "angry-defiant suicidal type." In contrast, the conformist suicidal girls are depressed and do not blame others for their depression. They are vulnerable to criticism and feelings of guilt, and rarely show delinquent or aggressive symptoms. Borst and Noam called these girls the "self-blaming suicidal type."

Clearly, treatment of these suicidal girls should take their level of psychological development into account. Not only do they present very different problems for the counselor, but different counseling strategies may be necessary for helping the two groups.

Erikson studied psychoanalysis, and his stage theory closely follows that proposed by Freud except that, first, he extended the description into adulthood and old age and, second, he focused on different desires and conflicts than those chosen by Freud.

Jane Loevinger (1977) has also proposed a sequence of eight stages:

1. Presocial: the task is to distinguish the self from what is nonself
2. Symbiotic: the task is to differentiate the self from the mother
3. Impulsive: the child acts impulsively in order to have an impact on the world

4. Self-protective: the child begins to learn the rules of the society
5. Conformist: the person begins to internalize the rules of the society
6. Conscientious: the person begins to develop a sense of morality
7. Autonomous: the person is marked by a heightened sense of identity
8. Integrated: the person integrates all of the conflicting desires and roles that have been developed.

In addition, a variety of stage descriptions have been proposed to address specific areas of development, such as moral development (Kohlberg, 1984) and cognitive development (Piaget, 1960a).

DISCUSSION

Major modifications to Freud's basic theory come from Jung's reconceptualization of the unconscious, from alternative classifications of desires, from debates as to which desires are the most basic, and from alternative proposals for the stages of human development. None of these, however, change the basic framework of Freud's comprehensive theory. Later chapters will discuss theories dramatically different from, although not necessarily incompatible with, Freud's theory.

II

THEORIES BASED ON COGNITION

4

George Kelly's Personal Construct Theory: A Theory of Cognition

George Kelly proposed a comprehensive theory of the way in which the mind thinks and makes decisions, that is, a theory of cognition that is relevant to personality (1955). First published formally in 1955, the theory quickly gained supporters, and now there is a journal devoted to the theory (the *Journal of Constructivist Psychology*).

George Kelly proposed a philosophical position for theories of all kinds, that is, all theories are tentative and should be modified when new evidence is collected. His own theory, however, quickly became established as gospel, and very few modifications to the theory have been proposed. This chapter first reviews his theory, and then, discusses a few recent thoughts about how the theory might be modified.

In his own book, Kelly presented his theory in a quasi-scientific manner, with formal postulates and corollaries, perhaps a result of his training in engineering. Although most textbooks follow this style of presentation, the theory is easier to follow if presented in a more conventional style.

THE BASIC ELEMENTS

In Freud's psychoanalytic theory, the basic elements of the mind are wishes. For Kelly, the basic elements are *constructs*. The notion of a construct is a little harder to grasp since we are not used to talking about and thinking in terms of them.

Consider three objects or events—let us say three friends of yours: Tim, Cindy, and Gene. Now ask yourself what do two of them have in common and how do they differ from the third? This is not a test in which the strategy is to find the simplest answer, such as, two have brown hair and one has blond hair. Your task is to consider how you think about people and what judgments you make about them. What personality traits affect your reactions to these three people? Perhaps Tim and Cindy are caring people, while Gene is uncaring. The dimension caring–uncaring is then one of your constructs.

Although we are accustomed to thinking about our desires, especially because so much of Freud's psychoanalytic theory has become part of general Western culture, we are not accustomed to thinking about our constructs. In order to find out what constructs people use, Kelly devised the role construct

GEORGE KELLY

George Kelly was born near Wichita, Kansas, in 1905. He was an undergraduate at Friends University in Wichita, Kansas, and Park College in Missouri, majoring in physics and mathematics (Maher, 1969). His interests changed, and he studied for a master's degree in educational sociology at the University of Kansas. After a variety of teaching jobs, he went to the University of Edinburgh in Scotland where he obtained a degree in education, after which he returned to the State University of Iowa for a doctorate in psychology, finishing in 1931.

He taught at Fort Hays Kansas State College until the Second World War and, after service as a psychologist during the war, was appointed professor and director of clinical psychology at Ohio State University. He retired in 1965 and moved to Brandeis University, but died the following year, in March 1966.

In discussing the development of his theory, Kelly noted that he found the behaviorist paradigm too simple to be of use and the psychoanalytic paradigm unscientific. Kelly attributed his switch from his early interest in physiological psychology to clinical psychology to the Depression and the obvious need to help those suffering.

The particular direction that his theory took was determined in part by the kinds of clients Kelly saw for counseling, who were mainly students. Kelly's theory was humanistic in tone and focused on the healthy aspects of our mind. However, his training in science and engineering influenced his view of what constitutes a sound scientific theory. Kelly phrased his theory in terms of postulates and corollaries, and he used terms such as grid and template.

Kelly's theory of the mind portrays individuals as "scientists" trying to build better and better theories of their world. He generalized this idea to theories of personality, proposing a philosophical principle that he called constructive alternativism, with the idea that all theories are tentative and should be changed over time to improve their accuracy of prediction and range of application. Ironically, those interested in Kelly's theory have proposed very few changes in it in the 40 years since its publication. Kelly, himself, did not always follow his own philosophy. In a seminar he gave in the last year of his life, Kelly one day proposed dividing the seminar into two groups, those for him and those against him. He was concerned that those criticizing his theory might affect the attitudes of those who liked the theory. He was persuaded not to do so by those who liked his theory. They told him that they welcomed the critical comments because his responses helped them better understand the theory.

repertory test (rep test), a simplified version of which is presented in the box on pages 44–45. If you complete it, you may discover what constructs are important to you at this point in your life.

A construct then is a quality or a feature that distinguishes some objects from other objects. It differs in an important way from terms such as concept or percept. Constructs are dichotomous. They have two *poles*, a *construct* and a *contrast*. It is unfortunate that Kelly used the term construct both for the dichotomous pair and for one of the poles of the dichotomous pair. This results in some difficulty in understanding his later definitions. In some places in his book, Kelly uses the term *likeness end* and *contrast* as names for the two poles, but he does not use them consistently.

All of the constructs that are in your mind form a *construction system*, and here we have the potential for introducing holistic concepts into the theory. However, Kelly remained primarily concerned with individual constructs, and so his theory is more appropriately viewed as atomistic.

People differ from one another in their construction systems, that is, in both their particular constructs and in the way they are arranged. When individuals encounter an event, they apply their construction systems to that event, that is, they *construe* it. Imagine that you see a person walking toward you, and they raise their hand. You apply your construction system, and you try to anticipate or predict what will happen next. You may classify the person as male, well-dressed, and looking friendly, in which case you predict that he is walking toward you to greet you. On the other hand, you may classify the person as male, dangerous, and unknown to you, in which case you may anticipate an attack.

Kelly formalized this process in his *fundamental postulate*—people's psychological processes and behaviors are determined by the way in which they anticipate events, that is, by the construction they place upon events. In the example above, if you construed the situation by anticipating a friendly greeting, you may have held out your hand to the man walking toward you. If you construed the situation by anticipating an attack, you may have fled in terror.

Kelly stated in his book that there is no motivation in his theory. It is not clear what he meant by this because the fundamental postulate is a motivational postulate. It explains why people choose one activity rather than another, a choice that constitutes the basic motivational issue that psychology has to explain.

A construction system, then, is rather like a scientific theory. We each have a theory of the world that we apply to the situations that we encounter. Each time, we find out whether our predictions were confirmed or not, and we take steps to make our theory of the world a better theory. Hopefully this theory, our construction system, will change and become a more accurate predictor of future events.

In particular, for people to interact meaningfully, they must be able to construe (understand) each other's construction system and, therefore, predict each other's behavior.

PROPERTIES OF THE POLES OF CONSTRUCTS

The poles of constructs have some interesting and important properties. For many people, one pole of their constructs may be used more than another. For example, if you are a suspicious person, you may classify more people as unfriendly as opposed to friendly. This pole is called the *emergent pole*. The other pole, which embraces fewer objects, is called the *implicit pole*, and if the implicit pole is rarely used, then it may be called *submerged*. The implicit pole is of special interest because we may have no name for it. We may apply the emergent pole to objects or events without ever being aware of what the contrast is. We may say, for example, that Mary and Alice are gentle but Jane is not.

I remember one person when I was a graduate student who often referred to people as intelligent. There were other people around who were never

THE REP TEST

To use George Kelly's repertory test, you list 22 people who play (or played) different roles in your life, including yourself, and then you produce 22 different constructs to describe these people. Kelly emphasized including people of both sexes, both relatives and friends, people you liked and disliked, and people who held power over you (such as teachers and employers) as well as people you had power over. His goal was to have a very diverse set of people on the rep test.

In order to illustrate the test here (Figure 4.1), list 12 friends and acquaintances whom you know at the present time. Be sure to include both men and women, as well as people you like and people you dislike. Write their names on the top of the grid. Then consider the three people indicated by the circles in the first row, those whose names appear in columns 1, 2, and 3. Think about these three people. What do two (any two of the three) of them have in common, and how do they differ from the third? Write the trait that the two have in common under the word construct and the trait that the third has in contrast under the word contrast on line 1. Then consider the trait listed under the word construct. Put a check mark in the square on line 1 under any of the 12 people who have this trait. We can assume then that any person not so checked has instead the trait listed under the word contrast.

Note that the task is to identify for yourself how you think about the people you know. The goal is not to complete the test as quickly as possible using any trait, trivial or not, that comes to mind. *Mary and Alan have blue eyes whereas Janet has green eyes* is not acceptable unless the color of the eyes of the people you know is really important in determining your reactions to them. Your task is to think about what traits are important to you in thinking about, discussing, and reacting to the people you meet.

Next, repeat this procedure for the three people indicated by the circles on line 2. And so on, 12 times. You will then have elicited 12 of your personal constructs.

Some of you may have difficulty thinking of 12 distinctly different construct–contrast pairs. That is not surprising. Often the same construct seems pertinent on several lines of the rep test, and sometimes two construct-contrast pairs are quite similar in meaning even though slightly different words are used to label them.

described as intelligent, but neither were they given any other label. After many years, I came across a paper written by this person that classified people as intelligent versus handicapped! Thus, handicapped was the implicit pole of the construct.

This illustrates the importance of asking people to name their own contrasts for their constructs. We cannot assume that we know the contrasts. For example, several people may have a construct in their construction system with one pole as *intelligent*, but they may differ in their contrasts. One may have *stupid* as the contrast, another may use *unintelligent*, and a third may use *irrational*.

Psychotherapists who use personal construct theory as one of their guides often spend time with clients making the implicit poles explicit. For example, suppose a client says *Everyone has been good to me*. What is the contrast of this statement? There are many possibilities: *whereas other people are mistreated*; *but I have not been good to them*; or *but will they continue to be good to me in the future*.

One clinical guideline suggested by Kelly is that clients fear that they would place themselves at the implicit or submerged poles of their constructs. Sub-

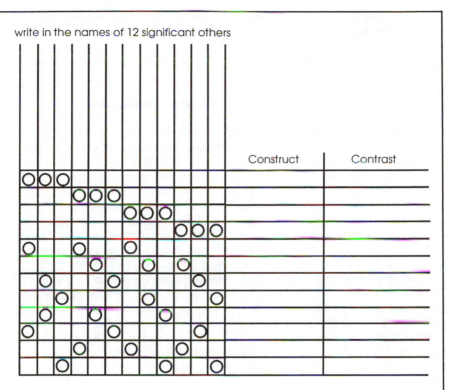

Figure 4.1　A simplified role construct repertory test.

merging the pole prevents them from testing and validating the accuracy and usefulness of those constructs as applied to themselves.

PROPERTIES OF CONSTRUCTS

Range and Focus of Convenience

A construct is not applied to every person or event. It applies to only some. Constructs may be irrelevant to some objects or not particularly useful. The construct *trustworthy–untrustworthy* may be usefully applied to adults but not to infants and children. The *range of convenience* refers to those objects or events to which the construct can be applied; the *focus of convenience* refers to those objects or events to which it is typically applied.

Superordinate and Subordinate Constructs

Not all constructs are equivalent. For example, one construct may be an element to be classified in another construct. Thus, constructs may be arranged hierarchically. *Superordinate* constructs may be more abstract than the *subordinate* constructs. For example, *intelligent–stupid* may be one element of a superordinate construct *the kind of person I like versus the kind of person I dislike*. Alternatively, one construct may have a larger range of convenience than another.

Permeable and Impermeable Constructs

A construct is *permeable* if it will admit to its range of convenience new elements that are not yet construed within its framework. A construct that will not admit new elements into its range of convenience is *impermeable*. However, in the examples Kelly gives for an impermeable construct, he describes a situation in which a construct will not admit new elements to *one pole* of a construct, which is not consistent with his definition. For example, Kelly (1955, p. 156) gives the following as an example of an impermeable construct: "If *ball* compromises certain things, then no other things can be balls. . . . These and only these are balls." This refers to only one pole of a construct, and so Kelly is giving here an example of an impermeable pole!

This confusion may result from using the term construct in two ways (for the total construct and for one pole of the construct). However, perhaps there is a need for two terms, one for a construct that does not permit any new elements to be classified at either pole, which is how Kelly defined the term (perhaps *impermeable construct*), and one for a construct that permits classification of new elements only at one pole (perhaps *impermeable pole*).

If we stick to Kelly's definition, an impermeable construct is one which is no longer applied to new objects of events. A few years ago, I used to be concerned with whether I could trust people. I asked friends how they defined trustworthy and how they dealt with untrustworthy people. I spent a great deal of time on this issue. Today, I ignore the issue completely. I no longer classify people as trustworthy or untrustworthy, and I no longer worry whether this person or that one will prove to be untrustworthy. The construct is now impermeable.

The meaning of a permeable construct changes as new objects are classified. Let us say that Mary and Alice are ambitious while Jane is not. Mary and Alice serve to define ambitiousness because it is a quality that they share. Now we meet Joyce whom we classify as ambitious and Annette whom we classify as not. The quality of ambitiousness has changed because now it is a quality shared by Joyce, Mary, and Alice. The meaning is now a little sharper than it was. Permeable constructs are, therefore, stable in the sense of being durable (they endure), but they are not necessarily rigid in meaning.

Propositional, Constellatory, and Preemptive Constructs

A *constellatory* construct is one that, after an object has been classified at one of the poles, has implications for how that object will be classified in other constructs. For example, Fred may be classified as a man, and for the person who so classified him, this may mean automatically, without further experience of him, that he is seen as aggressive, as using thinking more than feelings to make decisions, and as likely to be inappropriately sexual. His position in one construct fixed his position in a whole constellation of other constructs. Constellatory thinking is, therefore, stereotyped thinking. Racist, sexist, and ageist thinking is constellatory thinking. *Preemptive thinking* is even stronger for, once an object is classified in a preemptive construct, there is nothing more to say about it.

In contrast, *propositional* constructs classify objects without any implications for the object's position in other constructs. Fred is a man, but he may be a thinking or a feeling person. He may be aggressive, or he may be gentle.

Preverbal Constructs

Kelly recognized that children may develop constructs before they acquire a language, and so constructs may be *preverbal*. Since the concerns of children are probably centered around dependency, preverbal constructs may be concerned with these issues too. Preverbal constructs may be especially relevant to people's concept of themselves.

Core and Peripheral Constructs

Core constructs are those that are relevant to your identity, your sense of self, and your existence. *Peripheral* constructs are those that have less relevance to your sense of self. Psychotherapy typically has an impact on your core constructs; education has more of an impact on your peripheral constructs.

PROPERTIES OF CONSTRUCTION SYSTEMS

Suspended Sets of Constructs

Our construction system may have inconsistencies within it. If we view the construction system as a theory of the world, there may be subsystems or subtheories that apply only to some situations or on some occasions. For example, a scientist may believe that light travels in straight lines and also that light can be bent by gravity. When he designs an optical telescope or opera glasses, he may put aside his knowledge that light rays can be bent by gravity.

When you wake up depressed, you put aside your optimistic world view and, likewise, when you wake up happy, you put aside your pessimistic world view. In Kelly's terms, you have *suspended* one set of constructs while you operate on the other set. Some people may suspend one set of constructs more or less permanently, and it may require working with a psychotherapist to restore them to active functioning.

Tight and Loose Constructs

Kelly applied the terms tight and loose to individual constructs, but it makes more sense to apply them to sets of constructs. A *tight* set of constructs is one that leads to clear unambiguous predictions about an event. *Loose* sets of constructs lead to varying predictions. Freud's psychoanalytic theory is a loose scientific theory, whereas Skinner's paradigm of operant conditioning is a tight scientific theory. Conscious thinking is more likely to be tight, whereas dream processes are more likely to be loose. Perhaps nonpsychotic people think more tightly, whereas schizophrenics think more loosely?

WHAT HAPPENED TO FREUDIAN CONCEPTS?

New theories sometimes modify concepts developed by other theories and occasionally reject them. We, however, can often identify concepts from older theories in these new theories. Let us do this for some of Freud's psychoanalytic concepts.

The Unconscious

Kelly stated quite firmly that there was no unconscious in his theory. True, but there are concepts such as implicit and submerged poles, preverbal constructs, and suspended sets of constructs. Kelly defined a *level of cognitive awareness* that is highest when construing in socially acceptable symbols (such as your native language) and whose alternatives are readily accessible. A low level of cognitive awareness parallels Freud's notion of the unconscious, but it does, of course, have very different connotations and implications.

Defense Mechanisms

Several psychoanalytic defense mechanisms can be described using the terms of personal construct theory. For example, the simplest change a person can make in construing objects or events is to reclassify them from one pole of a construct into the other. If a person who was viewed as trustworthy is now viewed as untrustworthy, then our reactions to this person will be diametrically opposed now to what they once were. Thus, *reaction formation* is an easily chosen strategy in personal construct theory.

From the point of view of personal construct theory, *identification* is the reaction that occurs when an important figure in your life, say your mother, becomes one pole of a construct (*like my mother–unlike my mother*), you classify yourself at that pole, and that construct becomes one of your core constructs (that is, relevant to your sense of self).

Combined Concepts

Theorists are often reluctant to incorporate concepts from rival theories into their new theories. However, as impartial observers, we can do so. Thus, we can ponder what a "permeable wish" might be (a Kelly-Freud combined concept), or an "unconscious construct" (a Freud-Kelly combined concept). We must remember that theorists try to outline clear and often extreme positions.

In reality, each theory provides only some elements of the whole picture, and a complete theory will most likely one day incorporate all of the concepts and propositions put forth by a legion of theorists.

PROPERTIES OF THE PERCEPTUAL FIELD

The *perceptual field* is what we perceive. It is the information we receive from outside. We can open ourselves up to new experiences, even thrust ourselves into them, that is, we can *dilate* our perceptual field. Alternatively, we can close ourselves off from new experiences, and withdraw into a narrower world, that is, *constrict* our perceptual field. We can dilate or constrict in general, or only in specific areas.

The strategy a person chooses is designed to make the construction system work better. If we dilate our perceptual field, we are testing our construction system, our theory of the world, in more and more different and varied situations, and thus building a comprehensive theory of the world. For me, travel contributes to this. I have visited almost 50 countries in the last 15 years. People say that travel "broadens" the mind, and spatial metaphors are common in descriptions of the mind—the terms "well-rounded" and "narrow-minded," for example. It is hard to specify what broadening the mind means, but Kelly's theory explains it nicely. The people you meet in different countries who have different mannerisms and customs and who often do not speak your language force you to experiment, to test your construction system, and to modify it. I have walked past military tanks on the streets in Lima, Peru; visited Soweto, South Africa; helped my guide in Romania plan his defection from the totalitarian communist regime; and let a stranger in Africa take me from Senegal to Gambia. I have also touched mummified bodies in Dublin, Ireland; swum in hot springs around fallen Greek columns in Pammukale, Turkey; and played Scrabble with Filipino teenagers in the mountains of the Philippines. All of these experienes—traumatic, breathtaking, or intriguing—have "broadened" my mind.

Yet I also know people in southern New Jersey who rarely travel to Philadelphia and never to New York City. I knew one family whose members socialized only with relatives. These people constrict their lives, perhaps because they have found that their construction system does not function well in new settings or because they fear to put it to the test.

REDEFINING OLD TERMS

Readers coming to Kelly for the first time are often overwhelmed by the many new terms, each of which has a definition that has to be committed to memory. As we have noted before, Freud's psychoanalytic theory has been in existence for 90 rather than 40 years, and these ideas have found wide acceptance, so that its concepts have come into common usage. The concepts in Kelly's theory are not familiar to us.

However, Kelly also took common psychological terms and redefined them using the concepts of his theory. In some ways, this is the most provocative part of his theory for it makes us reconsider terms with which we thought we were familiar, but now realize we had not thought through fully.

Threat

Threat was defined by Kelly as an awareness that a comprehensive change was imminent in your core constructs, and thus in your conception of yourself. In the broadest sense, threat can be induced when we perceive any plausible alternative to our core constructs. For me, I often feel threat whenever I meet anyone who has devised a life style different from mine. My initial thought is often, "I ought to do that," though on reflection I realize that their choices are not for me. I have colleagues who earn extra money by consulting and some who do so by being psychotherapists. Ought I to do that too? No! I once had a colleague who had a wife and two children, two mistresses whose rents he paid, and several girlfriends; he had two full-time jobs and four part-time jobs. I had one wife, one child, no mistresses, and only one job. For a few hours, I felt that I was not making good use of my time! I have a colleague at my college who makes me feel like a dilettante. We both started akido together. He is now a black belt; I dropped out after a semester. I barely keep plants alive; he grows prize-winning orchids. I take photographs on my travels for my albums; he has exhibitions of his photographs. And so on. I explained Kelly's notion of threat to him one day as he was giving me a shiatzu massage. Of course, he has never written a book. Maybe I'm a threat to him?

In contrast, *fear*, defined as an awareness that a minor change is imminent in your peripheral constructs, is much less interesting.

Guilt

Guilt is defined as an experience that accompanies your perception that you have become dislodged from your core role. Your core role is the subsystem of constructs that enables you to predict and describe your behavior. It gives you a sense of identity. Guilt is the result of invalidating your core constructs, that is, finding out that you are not the kind of person whom you thought you were.

As a divorced parent who saw his son every weekend, I came to see myself as a rational and caring parent who treated his child with the same degree of respect and graciousness as I would have treated a beloved parent of my own. This became part of my self-image. I then became a step-parent, and I found much to my dismay that when I lived with children seven days a week I was an irrational and authoritarian parent who frequently flew into rages. I was not the kind of parent I had thought I was! I felt guilt in the sense that Kelly defined the term. Remember, the discrepancy between what you thought you are and how you now know you are has to be relevant to your *core* role for the guilt to be strong and psychologically important.

This definition of guilt is similar to that provided by Freudian psychoanalytic theory. For Freud, guilt is experienced when some of your desires come into conflict with your superego desires, desires that include the dos and don'ts (the ego ideal and conscience, respectively), most of which were introjected from your parents. For Kelly, guilt is experienced when your behaviors are not consistent with your theory of yourself. Although Kelly does not take a position on the sources of the core role, in particular, the degree to which is it formed by the expectations of the parents for their children, it is quite likely that many aspects of the core role are based on parental expectations for their children.

Anxiety

Anxiety is experienced when your construction system no longer applies to the situation that confronts you. You cannot construe (make sense of) what is happening. Finding yourself in any new situation leads to some anxiety. But if you have developed a sound construction system (theory of the world), you will eventually make sense of the situation and make effective choices as to how to respond. If you do this, your construction grows in its range of applicability.

However, if your construction system suggests no behavior for you, then your anxiety may become extreme and chronic. You may then choose several unhealthy strategies. For example, you may withdraw into a more predictable world (constriction), or you may loosen your construction system so that it provides some guidance, even though the decisions you make may be ineffective.

You can see that this definition of anxiety is very different from that provided by Freud's psychoanalytic theory. (For Freud, anxiety was experienced whenever a desire was deprived and whenever an unconscious desire was in danger of becoming conscious, see Chapter 2.) Indeed, the concept of anxiety can be seen as the critical concept in theories of personality. The way is which anxiety is defined often illuminates the theory quite well.

Aggression

Most of us commonly define people as aggressive when their behavior hurts us. Kelly, as in his discussion of other concepts, tried to look at this behavior from the subject's point of view. What is the aim of the aggressive person?

Kelly defined *aggression* as the active elaboration by people of their perceptual field. Aggressive people seek out and get involved in situations that require decisions and actions. The contrast of aggressiveness is *passivity*. Thus, aggressive sexual people seek out sexual situations and get involved sexually with others. Aggressive business people seek out business opportunities and actively pursue them. Other people may sometimes suffer as a result of the aggressive person's behavior. However, the goal is not to hurt others, but rather to get involved with and achieve in particular types of situations.

I have been aggressive in my research on suicidal behavior. I try to peruse everything published in the English language on the topic, and I have written or edited many books on suicide and many scholarly articles and notes. My behavior seems driven, but it harms no one.

Kelly suggested an interesting clinical hypothesis here, namely, that people are especially aggressive in areas that cause them anxiety, that is, which they cannot construe well. Because their construction system fails them in these situations, they explore the uncharted area in order to develop a better construction system to deal with the situations.

I have discussed with several of my colleagues in suicidology whether our interest in suicidal behavior and suicide prevention is a way of dealing with our own suicidal impulses. Interestingly, no active member of the American Association of Suicidology is known to have committed suicide. Perhaps intellectualization is a useful psychoanalytic defense mechanism (see Chapter 2).

Hostility

Suppose that you test a part of your construction system and find that it does not predict well what happened to you and so is of little use to you. This part of your construction system is invalid. What can you do? You could try to replace this part with a more useful construction system that anticipates the outcome of the events more accurately. If you do this, you are building a better construction system.

Alternatively you could refuse to accept the disconfirming evidence that has invalidated your construction system and, instead, seek to distort the information so that it is no longer inconsistent with your construction system, or you could even seek to extort information from the environment that is consistent with your construction system. These strategies are the essence of *hostility*.

Kelly chose Procrustes as his prototype of the hostile person. In Kelly's version of the ancient Greek myth, Procrustes was an inn-keeper who had a theory that every guest would fit his bed. Whenever he found a guest who was too short, Procrustes stretched him on a rack until he was long enough to fit the bed, usually killing him in the process. If the guest was too long for the bed, then Procrustes cut off parts of the guest until he too could fit the bed. In this way, i.e., by distorting the data, Procrustes maintained his theory that everyone fit his bed!

Thus, all of the defense mechanisms described in Freudian psychoanalytic theory are hostile maneuvers. They are ways of distorting evidence and, according to Kelly, they permit people to keep their theory of the world unchanged. The goal of hostile people is not to hurt others; it is to maintain their theory of the world unchanged.

Why should a person behave in a hostile manner? It seems easy to say in words, "Accept the evidence that your theory of the world is inaccurate and revise it," but in reality, this means an immense identity crisis. Most of us survived the identity crises of adolescence as we developed our core constructs and our overall theory of the world, but I am not sure we would want to go through such a crisis again, at least not without the help of a good psychotherapist.

Let me give an example of a hostile person. I came across a student once who had attempted suicide in strange circumstances—I'll call him Jim. It was vacation time on campus, and all of those students remaining on campus for the holiday were moved into one dormitory for convenience. Thus, since his roommate had gone home, Jim was with relative strangers. He took an overdose of his medication and told the others in the dormitory lounge what he had done. They showed little interest, and so Jim went off to bed to die. He woke up 48 hours later, at which point his roommate returned, found him, and took him to the campus infirmary. Jim told me that the overdose had not killed him because he had built up a tolerance to the medication during the time that he had been taking it. He had not allowed for this tolerance.

When telling me about this incident, he continually referred to the other students in his temporary dormitory who had let him die as "bastards," and he was very angry verbally about their indifference. Yet, at the same time, his face showed no sign of anger; instead he smiled and urged me to attempt suicide because it was an interesting experience!

After I scored the psychological tests that I had given him, I noticed that his score on the measure of resentment was higher than those of the others I had tested. Jim agreed strongly with statements such as "Not a day goes by without I meet someone I dislike," and "I get a raw deal out of life." My hypothesis, then, was that Jim had a very negative view of people. He constructed his suicide attempt so that he was surrounded by those who disliked him, and the one person who might have saved him was home. (I should point out that Jim had many negative qualities that did cause many people to dislike him.) These others rejected him, and this confirmed Jim's world view that other people could not be trusted and so truly merited his resentment. Jim attempted suicide in order to get rejected, that is, in order to confirm his view of the world. It was a hostile act, designed to extort evidence of rejection from others.

Kelly's System Principle

Chapter 6 discusses Andras Angyal's holistic theory of personality. One of the important concepts in Angyal's theory is that every system must have a guiding system principle, an abstract purpose or function for the system. Kelly's concepts of aggression, anxiety, and hostility provide the basis for what could be called his system principle.

From the definitions of those terms, it is clear that a healthy individual makes an effort to build a construction system that explains more and more of the world increasingly accurately. When our theory fails us we feel anxiety, and we try to develop constructs to explain those events that we cannot understand at present. We may even act aggressively in those areas. If we encounter disconfirming evidence that invalidates our construction system, then we revise the constructs. Thus, healthy people are always seeking to extend and refine their construction systems, that is, make them applicable to more of the world (extend them) and make them more accurate (refine them).

The unhealthy person, in contrast, when faced with anxiety, withdraws into a smaller, but more predictable, world and becomes passive and hostile.

PSYCHOLOGICAL PROCESSES

Finally, Kelly described two psychological processes that are commonly observed—the creativity cycle and the circumspection–preemption–control (CPC) cycle.

The Creativity Cycle

Creativity involves the ability to first think loosely and then tighten the constructs. The creative person can switch from loose to tight construing and back at will. Those who think loosely, but who can never tighten, are unable to communicate their ideas to others in a systematic way, and so they are often seen as eccentric or crazy. Those who can never loosen can think only in the ruts well established by earlier thinkers.

I once took my elderly mother (a very intelligent person but not formally educated) to the Tate Gallery in London, England, to see modern art. She viewed them with horror. "They look as if they've been painted by mental patients," she said, and there was some truth to her judgment. On reflection, I realized that some psychiatric patients can paint creatively, but they lack the ability to develop a style and to communicate to others what this style is. Creative people, on the other hand, can break the assumptions that people in their field make (loose thinking) and then build a good theory around the alternative assumptions (tight thinking). What if the earth revolved around the sun rather than the sun revolving around the earth? What if space was curved rather than straight? Rather than simply musing on these possibilities (loose thinking), scientists such as Galileo and Einstein built formal theories based upon these new ways of looking at the universe (tight thinking).

CPC Cycle

The circumspection–preemption–control (CPC) cycle is a decision-making sequence. When individuals encounter situations, they initially think propositionally. What is this? Is it this kind of situation or that? If it is that kind, what does this mean? We are unsure and ambivalent during this period of *circumspection*.

Then we classify it—we make a decision. We show *preemption*. A certain situation is of a particular kind that we have experienced before and whose development we can predict. Preemption gives us control because we now know how to behave in the situation in order to achieve what we want.

Impulsivity describes people whose period of circumspection is too brief. We judge that they preempted too quickly. The obsessive-compulsive person, on the other hand, takes much too long to make a decision. In that case, the period of circumspection is too long.

CONTENT OF CONSTRUCTION SYSTEMS

Kelly was not overly concerned with the *content* of construction systems, but rather with their *properties*. Thus, he did not propose general types of theories that people hold or specific constructs that people might have in common. Although Kelly did briefly mention *vague* and *superficial* constructs, others have considered the content of constructs in more detail. For example, Rohrer (1952) found that psychiatric patients who gave more psychological constructs on the rep test and fewer superficial ones improved more during psychotherapy.

DICHOTOMOUS VERSUS CONTINUOUS CONSTRUCTS

Kelly's decision to make constructs dichotomous has interesting implications. Kelly was adamant that when we classify a person or an event, we place the person at one of the poles of a dichotomous construct. This person is either friendly or unfriendly. How then can we say that one person is more friendly than another, since such a statement implies a continuous rather than a dichotomous scale? Kelly suggested several possibilities for this.

One possibility is that we view the person on many occasions. Let us say, for example, that we observe two people on each of 20 occasions. We classify Mary as friendly on 18 of the 20 occasions and Dave as friendly on seven of the occasions. Each time, we used a dichotomous classification system (friendly versus unfriendly), but Mary was judged friendly more often and so is a "friendlier" person than Dave.

An alternative possibility is that a particular judgment may be made up of several separate judgments. For example, the judgment of a person on the construct trustworthy–untrustworthy may comprise judgments on the constructs of moral–immoral, shows guilt–never shows guilt, honest–dishonest, and devious–straightforward. People then may have scores of trustworthiness ranging from 0 to 4 depending upon how they score on the four subordinate constructs.

Kelly's decision that constructs are dichotomous rather than continuous makes explanation of nondichotomous judgments about traits a problem for his theory.

DISTURBED BEHAVIOR

In general, Kelly took a holistic approach to psychiatric disorder by proposing general strategies for healthy and disturbed individuals. The healthy person tries to make more and more of the world predictable; the disturbed person withdraws into a more predictable world.

As you might expect, because Kelly rejected earlier theories of cognition when he proposed his theory, and because he redefined commonly used psy-

---

ARE PERSONAL CONSTRUCTS DICHOTOMOUS?

A basic assumption in George Kelly's theory of personal constructs is that our constructs are dichotomous. This means that we rate, for example, the people we know and whom we encounter in extreme terms, i.e., in all-or-nothing terms. Cromwell and Caldwell (1962) tested this assumption using a group of 44 undergraduate students enrolled in a course on introductory psychology. These students first rated 12 friends and acquaintances using their own personal constructs, elicited using a version of the rep test. The students also had to rate the same 12 friends and acquaintances using the personal constructs given by a different member of the group. For these two sets of ratings, the students were given lines 4.1 inches long and asked to make a mark on the line to indicate their judgment of the personality of the person being rated.

For the ratings made using their own personal constructs, the average rating of friends and acquaintances was 1.325 inches from the midpoint of the lines. (The maximum distance fromn the midpoint of the lines was 2.000 inches.) For the ratings made using someone else's personal constructs, the average rating of friends and acquaintances was 1.203 inches from the midpoint of the lines. This difference was statistically significant (on an analysis of variance, $F = 10.01$, $df = 1,42$, $p = .005$). Thus, Cromwell and Caldwell concluded that "rating behavior is more extreme when one uses his own rep test constructs, as compared to using the personal constructs derived from another person" (p. 45).

Note, however, that the difference in using one's own versus another's personal constructs, though statistically significant, was small. Furthermore, the ratings using one's own personal constructs were not as extreme as the ratings scales permitted, only 1.325 inches from the midpoint of the scales compared to the 2.000 inches possible.

---

chological terms (such as anxiety and hostility), he was not happy with the conventional terms for psychological disturbance. In particular, he disliked the classification of psychiatric disorders proposed by the American Psychiatric Association and formalized in the *Diagnostic and Statistical Manual*, revisions of which appear periodically.

Kelly preferred to conceptualize psychological disturbances in his framework. This means that he liked to talk of disorders of permeability, of loose construing, or of hostility and anxiety. However, one can see how some common psychiatric illnesses might be described in part using Kelly's theory.

For example, we might conceptualize the depressed person as constricting. Much of the depressed person's behavior seems to illustrate this—the apathy and lack of motivation, the loss of interest in eating and sexual behavior, the motor retardation, and so on. The depressed person often withdraws from the larger world. Suicide can be seen as the ultimate constriction. In bipolar affective disorder (which used to be called manic-depressive disorder), the person seems to swing from extremely constricted states (depression) to extremely dilated states (mania).

Schizophrenics may be seen as thinking loosely. Because their thinking is loose, it is not comprehensible to those with tighter thinking (especially those in the mental health profession guided by tight theories of the world in general and the causes of psychiatric disorder in particular).

The person with an obsessive-compulsive disorder (who used to be called the obsessive-compulsive neurotic), say the compulsive hand-washer who is afraid of getting infected from contaminated objects touched by others, can be seen as both constricted and as construing tightly. Because such people focus almost all of their attention on dirt and infection, they are constricted. In addition, they typically develop logical arguments to convince themselves that they might have become infected by germs and viruses from others and thus, should wash their hands once more—tight thinking.

CONSTRUCTIVE ALTERNATIVISM: A PHILOSOPHY

Kelly's view of the human mind is that the healthy person tries to build a better and better theory of the world, a process that involves testing assumptions, admitting disconfirming evidence, and revising the theory. He also raised this to a philosophical principle—*constructive alternativism*. Theories are built to be modified, and even destroyed, so that better theories can be devised.

Strangely, personal construct theory itself has shown little of this philosophy. Kelly's theory, as written down in 1955, has achieved the status of dogma. That version of the theory has become the "truth," and there has been less discussion and criticism of the original formulation and fewer alternatives proposed than is the case, say, for psychoanalysis, which in its longer history has developed all manner of variants, heresies, and alternatives. However, psychologists, following Kelly's ideology, should in the future feel free to propose alternatives to Kelly's theory and to modify his theory where to do so would improve its ability to predict the human mind.

COMMENTS

We have to be careful in reviewing Kelly's theory. It is not that George Kelly liked to mislead people, but he liked to test people, to play games, perhaps to see whether they were sharp enough to see the light. Part of this game playing is in the way in which he described his own theory. He noted very early in his exposition of the theory of personal constructs that his theory had no place for such concepts as learning, motivation, emotion, cognition, stimulus, response, ego, the unconscious, needs, reinforcement, and drive. Many readers of his theory accept this, and I can imagine Kelly's eyes twinkling as he says to himself, "Fooled you."

One task for any scholar who proposes a new theory is to show how this new theory is unlike any other that has been proposed before—to sharpen the differences rather than look for similarities. In his description of his theory above, Kelly is saying that his theory is not like Freud's psychoanalytic theory, and not like Skinner's theory of learning. But he is also misleading us.

No cognition? Almost all textbooks on theories of personality classify Kelly's theory as a cognitive theory because it deals with thinking and cognition. However, it was different from theories of cognition current at the time that Kelly developed his theory.

No motivation? Well, of course, there is no energy concept in Kelly's theory. However, the critical modern motivational issue concerns the choice of behavior—why this action rather than that action? Kelly's theory addresses this issue in many places, most clearly in his major principle—that people try to extend and refine their construction system, that is, to make choices that enable their construction system to make more accurate predictions about the world, and for healthy people, to make predictions about increasingly larger parts of the world.

Chapter 3 discussed Abraham Maslow's views on personality. Maslow, one of the founders of humanistic psychology, felt that psychologists focused too much of what he termed deficiency needs and not enough on growth needs— that is, on the fact that humans try to obtain objects they lack (such as food, security, esteem, and love) rather than on the fact that humans also like to play, are curious, and can in the right circumstances grow and become more fulfilled. Humanistic psychologists have not, on the whole, developed formal theories to cover growth needs, yet Kelly's theory is basically a theory of growth. The desire to build a better theory of the world is an intrinsic motivation in Kelly's theory, just as Maslow would require. Kelly noted that his theory could have focused on people's flight from anxiety (a deficiency-oriented approach), but he chose to state the theory from a growth perspective.

(In reviewing Kelly's book, Bruner, 1956, commented that, just as people were not the pigs that reinforcement theory—that is, Skinner's learning theory—would make of us, neither are they the professors that Kelly implies as a model! Bruner, therefore, saw Kelly's theory as a growth theory.)

No learning? Kelly's theory involves learning. People test their construction system in new situations and, if it does not perform well, modify it. This is learning, albeit not the simple kind of learning proposed by Skinner and other behaviorists.

No emotion? But Kelly does define threat, fear, anxiety, and guilt. Chapter 5 discusses how Prescott Lecky's theory provides definitions of love and happiness using a framework compatible with Kelly's theory.

Thus, Kelly's description of his own theory must be considered critically. Don't let him fool you.

One area in which Kelly's theory is weak is in the development of behavior. Kelly gave very little attention to the problem of why people developed particular types of constructs (such as *tight–loose*) and particular styles of behaving (such as *aggressive–passive*). He talked of what factors might underlie the choice at the moment of choice, but not what childhood events determined the adult choice of strategy. Kelly's theory is, therefore, a *phenomenological* theory, rather than an *etiological* theory. Because it focuses on the individual, it is *idiographic* in its approach, a term coined by Gordon Allport (1962) to describe an approach that describes a person's unique individuality rather than assessing someone in relation to others. Indeed, Kelly's role construct repertory test may be the only truly idiographic psychological test ever devised.

Recent work on personal construct theory has focused mainly on research using the psychological test he devised, the rep test (Adams-Webber, 1979), and on the therapeutic implications of the theory (Neimeyer, 1993). However,

Adams-Webber (1970) suggested a developmental sequence for the evolution of construct systems, involving first differentiation of alternative substructures, independently organized, followed by their integration into a hierarchical scheme. Adams-Webber noted that his proposal was similar to the ideas of both Werner (1957) and Piaget (1960b). Werner suggested an orthogenetic principle in which cognitive development moves from states of relative undifferentiation and global structures to increasing differentiation and hierarchical integration. Piaget, too, argued that cognitive schemata move from differentiation to integration at increasingly higher levels of abstraction.

Adams-Webber noted that extremes in this process can be pathological. On the one hand, construction systems can become so fragmented in structure that it will be impossible for individuals to relate one aspect of their experience to another and, thus, no longer function as an operational whole. On the other hand, construction systems can become so tightly organized that all constructions of events will come down to classification using one major construct. Progressive differentiation and reintegration prevents these extremes from occurring.

Modern personal construct scholars are developing Kelly's ideas and extending the theory into new arenas. The following chapter explores how other personality theorists have proposed concepts similar to those in Kelly's theory and applied them to areas and issues that Kelly neglected.

5

Cognitive Theories: Alternative Views

Many other cognitive theories of the mind have been proposed, although none have the comprehensiveness of Kelly's theory. Some theorists have rephrased Kelly's ideas in different and more heuristic manners, and some have extended Kelly's ideas. This chapter reviews these alternative viewpoints.

LEON FESTINGER

The basic elements in Festinger's (1957) theory of cognitive dissonance are cognitions, that is, knowledge of the things that you know about yourself: your behavior and your surroundings. Cognitions include opinions, beliefs, attitudes, and values. Your elements of cognition map reality for you.

Two cognitions may be irrelevant to each other. You may be aware that it takes 4 weeks for mail to get from New York to Paris by sea and that a dry, hot July is good for crops in Iowa. These two cognitions seem to be irrelevant. However, it is often difficult to be quite sure that they are irrelevant. For example, what if an Iowa farmer is on vacation in Paris?

Two cognitions may also be relevant to each other. Two cognitive elements are *consonant* if one implies the other. Two cognitive elements are *dissonant* if one implies the opposite of the other. For example, dissonance may have a logical basis (you may believe that man will reach the stars soon, but you may also be aware that it will take too long for the journey), a cultural/mores basis (it is improper to pick up a pork chop bone in a restaurant, but your particular bone is proving hard to eat with a knife and fork), a specific/general basis (you are a Republican, but you prefer the Democratic candidate), or a past experience basis (you are standing out in the rain, but you are not getting wet).

Dissonance is greater the more important the cognitive elements involved are in your behavior. Dissonance is also greater the more elements that are incompatible with one of your cognitive elements. The maximum possible dissonance between two elements equals the total resistance to change of the less resistant element.

Cognitive dissonance leads to a motivation to reduce the dissonance. The more dissonance you have in your cognitive elements, the stronger your motivation. People are always striving toward consistency within themselves, and the presence of inconsistency is motivating. We can see immediately that this focus on consistency is very similar to George Kelly's theory of personal constructs and to Prescott Lecky's theory reviewed later in the chapter.

Remember that most of our cognitive elements are consistent. We believe that a college education is good, and we encourage our children to go to college. But when inconsistencies exist they can be dramatic. Some people may think blacks are as good as whites, yet do not want blacks in their neighborhood. Some people may believe in public education and yet send their own children to private schools.

How do we reduce cognitive dissonance?

1. We can change our behavior relevant to one of the cognitions. For example, we smoke and we realize that smoking increases our chances of lung cancer, which we want to avoid. We can stop smoking.
2. We can change an environmental cognitive element. For example, you may prefer to be a hostile person and so you surround yourself with people who clearly deserve your hostility. Or if you are a smoker, as in our previous example, you may avoid nonsmokers and associate only with smokers.
3. We can add a new cognitive element. If you are a smoker, you may read material critical of research on smoking and lung cancer. You may note that many more people die from car accidents than from lung cancer. When I was told to cut down on cholesterol, I was reluctant to do so because I liked high-cholesterol foods so much. Thus, I tried to find evidence that the cholesterol one ingested was not relevant to the cholesterol level in the blood.

   This new cognitive element may directly reconcile two dissonant elements. For example, the Ifaluk who dwell in Micronesia, believe that people are good. But their children go through a period of rebellion during which they are hostile and destructive. The Ifaluk could change their beliefs. They could come to believe that people are bad or that aggression is good. Rather, they have come to believe in malevolent ghosts that enter into (and "possess") people and cause them to behave badly (Spiro, 1953).
4. Finally, we can avoid dissonant information. The smoker can avoid noticing the warnings on cigarette packs, avoid nonsmokers, and avoid reading articles describing the connection between smoking and lung cancer.

However, we are resistant to change. If we change a behavioral element, the change may involve loss and pain. The behavior satisfied some of our needs, and giving up the behavior may lead to deprivation of these needs. I like eggs. The smoker gets gratification from his smoking. Often a behavioral change is not possible.

If we try to change an environmental element, we may have difficulty in finding persons to support our position. Smokers are under heavy attack these days and find nonsmokers everywhere and restrictions on smoking in many places. Finally, if we change a cognitive element, we may eliminate its dissonance with one other cognitive element, but we may create a new dissonance with some third element. Our system of cognitive elements is often complexly interrelated.

Cognitive dissonance is always aroused when we make a choice between two alternatives. The positive aspects of the alternative we rejected and the negative aspects of the alternative we chose create dissonance. If the choice is between two relatively unimportant objects, such as which film to on a given

A RESEARCH STUDY ON COGNITIVE DISSONANCE

According to cognitive dissonance theory, cognitive dissonance is generated whenever a person makes a choice. The negative features of the chosen object and the positive features of the rejected object create dissonance over the choice. How might an individual deal with this dissonance?

Ehrlich, Guttman, Schönbach, & Mills (1957) explored this by studying car advertisements read by people who had just bought a car. They argued that new car owners would read the advertisements about the car they had bought more than the cars they rejected. This tactic would support their choice because they would read about the good features of the car they had just purchased and avoid reading about the good features of the cars they rejected. In contrast, people who had owned their car for many years would not show this trend.

In the Minneapolis region, 125 male residents were interviewed and shown issues of the newspaper and the popular magazines they subscribed to and asked whether they noticed each car advertisement and whether they had read it (Table 5.1).

Table 5.1 Noticing and reading ads by car owners

	Car owned	Cars considered but rejected
Noticed ad		
New car owner	70%	66%
Old car owner	66%	52%
If noticed ad, read it		
New car owner	67%	39%
Old car owner	41%	45%

The results supported the prediction. There was no difference in whether new car owners noticed the advertisements for the car they purchased or the cars they rejected, but the new car owners were much likely to read about the car they purchased than about the cars they rejected.

There has been criticism of the methodology used in the research conducted on cognitive dissonance theory, and alternative explanations have been proposed for the phenomena identified (Chapanis & Chapanis, 1964).

night, then the amount of dissonance is small. But if the choice is between two important objects, such as which lover to marry, then the amount of dissonance may be great.

Stice (1992) argued that cognitive dissonance is very similar to guilt; therefore, they may be analogous concepts. Stice noted that both dissonance and guilt are negative emotional states; they both require the person to feel personally responsible (for the counter-attitudinal behavior or the desire); and they both can be relieved by such tactics as distorting memories, performing some self-affirming act, intoxication, and confession.

Discussion

Many of the tactics that people use to reduce dissonance are similar to Kelly's concept of hostility versus realistic acceptance (distorting and accepting information versus changing an element to be consistent with the data). It is interesting that Festinger's phrasing of the idea stimulated a great deal of research (see the accompanying box for an example), whereas Kelly's phrasing of the idea has not. Thus, we can see that the choice of terms and their connotations have important consequences.

PRESCOTT LECKY

Lecky (1969; first published in 1944) argued that humans are units, i.e., systems that operate as a whole. Humans are always active; we need to explain only the choice of activity. Lecky felt that such dynamic systems can have only one purpose, one source of motivation, and he proposed the need for unity or self-consistency as this universal dynamic principle.

Conflict is a result of the environment altering the system. The system then tries to eliminate this conflict. Personality is an organization of values that are consistent with one another. The individual always tries to maintain his integrity and unity of the organization, even when we judge his behavior to be irrational or disturbed. This organization defines his role, furnishes him with standards, and makes his behavior appear regular. Lecky saw individuals as having two tasks: (a) maintaining what he called "inner harmony" within their minds, that is, an internally consistent set of ideas and interpretations, and (b) maintaining harmony between their minds and the environment, that is, between their experience of the outside world and their interpretations of this experience.

Chapter 6 discusses how these aspects of Lecky's theory are similar to Angyal's. Both theories are holistic and see the mind as a dynamic organization. Lecky proposed one system principle; Angyal, two. Both view organism–environment interactions as fluid, with neither the organism nor the environment cast as the subject or the object. Yet, in his choice of a system principle that focused on consistency, Lecky foreshadowed the cognitive theory of Kelly.

For Lecky, learning was a process of assimilating new experiences. As the person assimilates these experiences and maintains his organization in a greater variety of situations, he maintains his independence and sense of freedom. Psychological development is a process of assimilating new information so as to maintain a self-consistent organization of values and attitudes. Whereas learning serves to resolve conflict, conflict must always precede learning. Conflict may profitably be viewed as a clash between two modes or ways of organizing.

We need to feel that we live in a stable and intelligent environment. We need to be able to foresee and predict environmental events and, by anticipating them, prevent sudden adjustments. Anxiety is caused by breakdowns in our predictive system. To do this we may have to avoid certain situations or make overly simplistic judgments, but the goal is self-consistency. For some individuals, preservation of their predictive system without change becomes a goal in itself, and they seek experiences that confirm their predictions and avoid situations that disconfirm their predictions. This definition of anxiety is identical to that of Kelly, and the strategy here is a hostile maneuver.

Lecky brought emotions into his theory in a way consistent with Kelly's ideas but extending them. *Love* was defined as the reaction toward someone who has already been assimilated and who serves as a strong support to your idea of self (in Kelly's theory, your core constructs). Grief is an emotion experienced when your personality must be reorganized due to the loss of one of its supports. Hatred and rage are emotions felt toward unassimilatable objects (that is, events which you cannot construe). Horror is the emotion felt when we are confronted with experiences that we are not prepared to assimilate, such as a ghastly accident. Experiences that increase consistency and unity give rise to joy and pleasure. If your behavior violates your self-concept, you feel guilt (that is, you have become dislodged from your core role). Fear is experienced when we fail to resolve inconsistencies.

Let us look at pleasure in more detail. Pleasure is experienced when we master new experiences, for example, when we learn to like olives or bitter coffee. If we could learn to tolerate more bitter substances than coffee, other pleasures would replace our liking for coffee. The same is true for other sensory modalities. For example, as we mature, we come to like more and more complex music, art, and literature. The more difficult an accomplishment, the more pleasure we derive from it. Pleasure is clearly related to the basic desire for unity or self-consistency, and it can be understood only historically. Pleasure came into existence because of a difficulty that was overcome, and continuous pleasure demands continuous solution of new problems.

Lecky noted that everyone's behavior is logical to them, in their system. If a person's behavior seems illogical to us, it is not because the person is irrational, but because we do not understand. We do not understand because their definitions and attitudes do not resemble ours. This is very similar to Kelly's sociality corollary.

Lecky explored the relationship between his concepts and psychoanalytic terms. Identification is the child's attempt to unify his self-concept and his view of his parents. He assimilates and imitates them and adopts their opinions and attitudes. Most parents also identify with the child and make themselves more assimilatable by taking over some of the child's standards. Resistance is a response of an organism resisting reorganization. It is a natural device and not a symptom of neurosis. If people were able to change too easily, they would have no personality. If events occur too rapidly, assimilation and change may be impossible. The person must then choose between disorganization or avoidance of the environmental input.

Emotions were seen by Lecky as characteristic of behavior when first encountering a new problem. They are, in fact, a way of assisting the acquisition of control over the experience and, when the experience is assimilated, the emotion will be reduced. Emotions do not disorganize behavior. The new experience disorganizes the behavior, or rather the personality, which in turn leads to less stereotypy in the person's behavior.

Lecky noted that as we develop, we assimilate more and more experiences and a spatial metaphor becomes applicable. The field of normal behavior grows at the expense of abnormal behavior. The metaphor is present in such common terms as *broad-minded* and *well-rounded* and the theories of Alfred Adler (action circles) and Kurt Lewin (life space).

Discussion

Lecky's theory of personality was not well-developed at the time of his death. It can be seen that it is consistent with the ideas of both Angyal (Chapter 6) and Kelly (Chapter 4). In some ways, it stresses holistic, dynamic, and organizational principles and so resembles Angyal's theory. In other ways it focuses upon cognitive structures and the need for consistency in these structures and so resembles Kelly's personal construct theory. Lecky's theory has historical interest but adds no new concepts to the basic theory of personality. However, the theory extends Kelly's theory to new areas, such as love and pleasure.

LARS-GUNNAR LUNDH

Lundh (1983) is primarily a cognitive psychologist and concerned with topics in thinking and memory. However, his ideas have some congruence with cognitive theories of personality. Lundh has proposed that the mind might usefully be conceptualized as a system of *meaning structures*.

Lundh introduced the concept of a meaning structure to explain the fact that people perceive the same situations and events differently. Events have a different meaning for each of us. Our meaning structures are the structures through which we perceive the world. They are mainly cognitive, but also have affective components. They include knowledge, beliefs, emotions, and motives. (Lundh saw his concept as similar to Kurt Lewin's "life space"—see Chapter 9—but Lewin's concept refers to the complete system of meaning structures.) Meaning structures develop as a result of both genetic dispositions and learning.

Meaning structures determine what perceptual information we expect and take in; they are modified as a result of new experiences. Lundh noted that these functions corresponded to Piaget's concepts of assimilation and accommodation, respectively, which are described in a following section.

Because remembering the past is achieved by means of our present meaning structures, and our meaning structures have changed from our early ones, it is difficult (if not impossible) to recollect original experiences exactly as they occurred.

Although Lundh included affective and motivational components in a meaning structures, he treated meaning structures as primarily cognitive. For example, if we are hungry, Lundh noted that our perception of a situation will be affected both by our meaning structures and our hunger (a motivational state). Thus, hunger is an element outside of meaning structures.

Lundh noted that events and objects may be more or less affectively charged to the observer. Lundh saw Freud's *cathexis* (in the traditional sense of the word) and Kurt Lewin's *valence* (see Chapter 9) as terms referring to this process. Objects that are more affectively charged are more meaningful to the observer, that is, they have a stronger significance.

Meaning structures can be activated by external stimuli or by internal stimuli from the mind. They can be activated consciously or unconsciously. Indeed, several can be activated simultaneously, with the consciously activated ones forming the figure and the unconsciously activated ones the ground. When a meaning structure is activated, we may be said to have a particular mental set.

If we know (or understand) the meaning structures of someone else, then we can feel empathy for them. This notion corresponds quite closely to what Kelly called his sociality corollary.

Mental illness was seen by Lundh as a pathology in the meaning structures. Lundh did not discuss these pathologies in detail. However, he noted a few possibilities. Meaning structures can lose their affective elements. Nothing then would be reinforcing, and the meaning structures would become lifeless cognitive structures. These states seem to resemble the states of depression and apathy. A meaning structure may no longer be applicable, for example, when a person tries to cope with double-bind communications from a parent. If our meaning structure no longer applies to a situation (a situation similar to Kelly's concept of anxiety), then we may well develop learned helplessness.

Lundh noted that meaning structures can be connected to one another horizontally, forming propositional structures—if this, then that. The propositional structures represent our habitual ways of thinking about empirical matters and our system of logic. Meaning structures can also be arranged vertically, leading to conceptual structures that are not open to empirical testing but that organize the meaning structures.

As a cognitive theorist, Lundh's ideas are quite similar to those of other cognitive theorists, such as Kelly and Piaget. His theory, as a theory of the mind, is not at all well articulated, but clearly his theory is compatible with concepts proposed by these other cognitive theorists.

PAUL McREYNOLDS

The central process for Paul McReynolds (1956, 1960) was the way in which we perceive the world. Behaviors are energized and directed by tendencies to obtain and avoid certain kinds of perceptions. The basic conceptual units are called *percepts*, the elements that pass through the mind, some of which we are aware of and some of which remain outside our awareness. Mental life consists of two processes: (a) obtaining and receiving percepts, and (b) assimilating or integrating them. This double process is called *perceptualization*.

There are two sources of percepts. Some are received by chance. They are thrust upon us. The second source is actively seeking some percepts, especially new or novel percepts. McReynolds proposed that there was a natural tendency to seek and experience new percepts. This tendency was innate, but modified by early experiences.

In assimilation, percepts enter harmoniously and congruently into systematic conjunction with percepts that were experienced previously and have already been incorporated into the apperceptive mass. The percepts are assimilated into *conceptual schemata*, which can be seen as relatively enduring plans or programs for the ordering of percepts (c.f., Kelly's construction systems). Assimilation involves classifying or categorizing percepts.

Some percepts fit into existing schemata easily. Others require *construction* or *restructuring* of the schemata. (In psychotherapy, this restructuring is called *working through*.) Restructuring often requires further percepts before the first percept can be assimilated. Some percepts are difficult to assimilate (and some schemata are difficult to utilize for assimilation). Contradictions, anomalies, and discordances can exist among percepts and schemata. (This is similar to Kelly's notion of inconsistency within construction systems and Festinger's notion of cognitive dissonance.) As percepts are assimilated, they modify the schemata a little.

People have a tendency to find schemata incongruent with reality to be unsatisfactory. In time, people tend to restructure their schemata so as to bring them in closer accord with the real world, as both Kelly and Lecky have proposed.

The more percepts assimilated into a schema, the greater the stability of that schemata and the stronger its resistance to restructuring. However, if the number of percepts incongruent with a schema grows large enough, the schema may become untenable, resulting in its rejection, making the previously assimilated percepts now unassimilated. Conceptual schemata are sometimes organized into more inclusive conceptual systems.

Perceptualization has a typical rate for each person, which may be called the optimal rate (c.f., Freud's concept of the rate of cathexis). The emotion associated with this rate is pleasure. A higher rate is exciting and a lower rate boring. Perceptualization is not an instinct or a motive. It is simply something that the mind does, much as the stomach digests food.

The rate of perceptualization varies from moment to moment in a person. The process of obtaining new percepts and the process of assimilating them tend to keep pace. McReynolds proposed a homeostatic mechanism also, in which the perceptualization rate rebounds after a previous low period, and vice versa. McReynolds also accepted individual differences in the perceptualization rate, possibly as a function of intelligence, personality, or life experiences.

A motive is a tendency to obtain or avoid percepts of a given type. In particular, if there are unassimilated incongruent percepts in the mind, then the person will seek out percepts that might help resolve the incongruence and facilitate assimilation of the percepts. This is an *incongruence motive*. Individuals are also motivated to seek out new percepts simply to keep the perceptualization rate optimal, i.e., *perceptualization motives*. The particular kind of percept sought varies with the individual.

Perceptualization motives, compared to incongruence motives, are less focalized, are more amenable to replacement with substitute motives, are more often associated with pleasure (rather than relief), and are preceded by feelings of boredom (rather than anxiety). McReynolds saw a rough parallel here with Maslow's growth and deficiency motivation.

Anxiety

Percepts that are incongruent with percepts already perceived are difficult to assimilate. If they remain unassimilated, we experience ambivalence. Unassimilated percepts accumulate and cause anxiety. (The nature of the percepts could possibly affect the level of anxiety too, but McReynolds decided to ignore this possibility.) New percepts can also affect previously assimilated percepts and thereby change the level of anxiety drastically.

Four factors make percepts difficult to assimilate.

1. A rate of influx of percepts too high
2. The percepts are too novel to assimilate
3. The additional percepts needed to assimilate the present percepts are not presently available
4. The percepts are incongruent with one another or with the schemata.

The first three sources will disappear with time, but the fourth source may generate long-term anxiety.

McReynolds noted several hypotheses that could be derived from these ideas. First, the greater a person's anxiety the stronger should be his tendency to assimilate new percepts that cannot be avoided (c.f., Kelly's tactic of loose construing). This will prevent his level of anxiety rising still further. Second, the more anxious a person is, the more he should resist giving up a conceptual schema according to which percepts have been assimilated. To give up a schema would result in more unassimilated percepts and raise the anxiety level still higher. Third, anxious persons should tend to deny or avoid the perception of incongruent stimuli (c.f., Kelly's strategy of hostility). (McReynolds noted that the person did not have to be aware of the incongruencies for this to happen.)

McReynolds noted that normal and pathological anxiety are the same because both arise from unassimilated percepts. The only differences are those of degree and of coping strategies necessary. When unassimilated percepts are relatively assimilatable, we experience thrill, but when they are not we experience anxiety.

Trauma leads to anxiety because it results in percepts that are not readily assimilatable. Sometimes, new percepts destabilize earlier experiences (and schemata), resulting in a flood of now unassimilated percepts. Psychotherapy seeks to reverse these processes by helping the patient to assimilate previously unassimilated percepts and to reintegrate perceptual systems that were incongruent with other systems.

Schizophrenia and Neurosis

McReynolds applied his theory to schizophrenia. Schizophrenia was hypothesized to be due to extremely high levels of unassimilated percepts. This

SCHIZOPHRENICS AS AUGMENTERS

This chapter discussed McReynolds' view that schizophrenics may have high levels of anxiety because they have too many unassimilated percepts. One cause of a high number of unassimilated percepts may be that the stimuli impinging upon the individual are too intense, and this intensity makes assimilation of the percepts difficult. For example, compare your appreciation of a professor's lecture if the professor is shouting rather than talking with a normal volume.

Petrie (1967) conducted some studies of schizophrenics that support this particular hypothesis. She was interested in whether people underestimated or overestimated the "intensity" of stimuli. She used two tasks, estimating the size of an object explored with the hand while blindfolded and the pain threshold, for example, to heat. She found that some people overestimated the size of objects and were relatively sensitive to pain, and she called these people *augmenters*. She found others who underestimated the size of objects and were relatively insensitive to pain, and she called these people *reducers*.

Seventeen schizophrenics were allowed to handle a block 2.5 inches wide with one hand while blindfolded. Then they were required to handle a block only 1.5 inches wide with one hand, still blindfolded, while they estimated its width with the other hand using a tapered block.

On the first test, 83% of the schizophrenics reduced and 18% augmented. After 24 hours, 83% of the schizophrenics reduced and 18% augmented. Thus, it appears that schizophrenics are reducers.

However, Petrie noted an odd feature of the performance of these schizophrenics that she deemed important. The augmenters on the first testing occasion became reducers on the second, whereas the augmenters on the second occasion had been reducers on the first occasion. This led Petrie to an intriguing hypothesis. She suggested that schizophrenics are basically augmenters but, since augmenting makes stimuli too intense to bear, schizophrenics erect reducing defenses that cut down the perceived intensity of the incoming stimuli. However, these defenses break down from time to time. Thus, when a researcher comes in to the hospital to test the performance of the schizophrenics, a small percentage have lost their ability to reduce the intensity of incoming stimuli and, therefore, appear to be augmenters. On a different occasion, however, a still small but different percentage have temporarily lost their ability to reduce the intensity of incoming stimuli. Schizophrenia may, therefore, be in part a defensive maneuver adopted by some people who are extreme augmenters.

high level of unassimilatable percepts in schizophrenics may result from constitutional tendencies, such as the augmenting tendency proposed by Asenath Petrie (1967). Schizophrenia may result from the receipt of unassimilatable percepts from parents, from the double-bind communications proposed by Weakland (1960), or from other sources.

High levels of unassimilated percepts and accompanying anxiety can predict the common symptoms of schizophrenia. If the schizophrenic has a high level of unassimilated percepts, he will avoid new percepts. Thus, the schizophrenic will withdraw, particularly from situations that yield percepts in his own unique area of incongruence (and then appear apathetic, and in extreme cases, catatonic). However, to keep his perceptualization rate optimal, he may have to engage in idiosyncratic kinds of interests and activities, which may make him appear odd to others. Such patients appear to have difficulties in organized and directed thinking.

Withdrawal may lead to situations similar to sensory deprivation. Thus, hallucinations result as a way for the mind to generate percepts to keep the perceptualization rate optimal. The deficit in organized and directed thinking makes discrimination of hallucinated percepts from external percepts difficult.

Delusional beliefs can be seen as schemata devised to assimilate some of the unassimilated material. In order to maintain his delusional schema in the light of reality, the schizophrenic has to avoid percepts inconsistent with his delusional schemata and seek percepts congruent with it (c.f., hostility in Kelly's theory).

Furthermore, to assimilate percepts, the schizophrenic may resort to using loose and lax criteria for classifying and categorizing percepts so that he can assimilate some of them. Thus, percepts may be assimilated in ways that others do not understand or accept. This will make communication with the schizophrenic difficult, and we will judge his thinking to be disorganized.

Neurosis too is a result of unassimilated percepts. However, the quantity of unassimilated material is less in neuroses than in psychoses.

Discussion

McReynold's discussion of anxiety extends Kelly's ideas about the same concept. In particular, McReynolds discusses in detail the different sources of anxiety and applies the ideas to schizophrenia, areas that Kelly neglected.

GEORGE MILLER, EUGENE GALANTER, AND KARL PRIBRAM

Behavior is temporal. It is a sequence of motions. It has a pattern that flows. How may this pattern be described? Miller, Galanter, and Pribram (1960) formulated a theory of cognition based on two major concepts: images and plans. For example, you imagine what you day is going to be like, and you make plans to cope with it.

A *plan* is a hierarchical process in the organism that can control the order in which a sequence of operations is to be formed. It is like the program for a computer. The molar units in the organization of behavior are called the *strategy*; the molecular units, the *tactics*. Typically only one plan is executed at a given time, though rapid alternation between plans is possible. Plans can be conscious or unconscious. The *image* includes all the accumulated, organized knowledge that the organism has about itself and its world. *Values* are part of the image.

The basic unit described by Miller and his associates is the test, operate, test, out (TOTE) unit (Figure 5.1). Action is initiated by perception of an incongruity between the state of the organism and the state that is being tested for. The action persists until the incongruity is removed.

Miller noted that the arrows in the TOTE unit might represent energy, information, or control (for example, the order in which instructions are to be executed). The feedback arrow in the TOTE unit is a stimulus, information

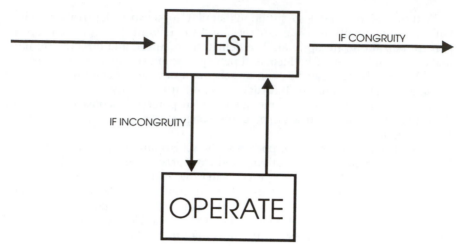

Figure 5.1   A diagram of a TOTE unit.

(for example, knowledge of results), or control (for example, instructions). The feedback allows comparison and testing.

The TOTE unit represents the basic pattern in which our plans are cast. The TEST phase involves the specification of whatever knowledge is necessary for the comparison to be made, that is, the image. The operation phase represents what organism does about it. Thus, the TOTE unit involves action, a feature that seems lacking in Kelly's personal construct theory.

TOTE units can be arranged hierarchically. The operational phase of a higher-order TOTE unit might itself consist of a string of other lower-order TOTE units, and so on. We can have plans to coordinate plans and plans to construct plans (so called metaplans). Miller and his associates used hammering a nail to illustrate a very simple TOTE unit (Figure 5.2).

Intention indicates that a person has begun the execution of a plan (or is about to begin it). It typically refers to the uncompleted parts of a plan whose execution has already begun. A *motive* has two components: a value and an intention. *Value* refers to the image and the *intention* refers to the plan.

Miller and his associates noted that plans are always being executed as long as we are alive. The question is not "Why are plans executed?" but rather "Which plans are executed?"

Miller and his associates conceptualize *instincts* as plans for behaviors that are inherited. (It is the plan, not the behavior, that is inherited.) *Habits* and *skills* are plans that were originally voluntary but that have become relatively inflexible, involuntary, and automatic. Plans may be involuntary (that is, they cannot be changed depending upon the consequences for the organism) and inflexible (the component parts of the plan cannot be rearranged or reordered).

Often people group together to execute a public plan based on a public image. If the public plan is continually repeated, then the sub-plans that are carried out by each member of the group involve division of labor and respon-

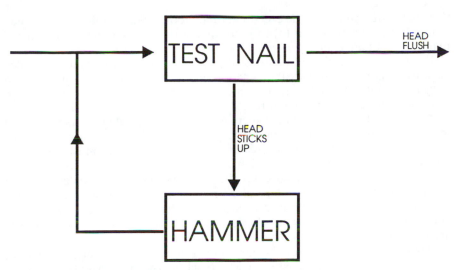

Figure 5.2   A TOTE unit for hammering a nail.

sibility, which define a set of *roles*. A person's role, therefore, is defined in terms of the plans that he is expected to execute in the group.

Psychopathology

The coordination of plans is done through other plans, higher up the hierarchy, which themselves are TOTE units. People often carry out several plans at the same time. We coordinate several plans into a single stream of behavior. Occasionally, two plans may be incompatible. To discover this may raise difficulties and involve revising the image. If the two plans are incompatible and isolated from each other, they are never compared or contrasted with each other, and in extreme cases may result in a multiple personality. Neurotic conflict may involve the possession of two incompatible plans that are quite pervasive and where the abandonment of either is impossible. (For example, one plan may have been accepted from the mother and one from the father.) No act may advance both plans. So the person shows indecision, vacillation, or inaction.

Can people ever be planless? Deep sleep, anesthesia, and concussion come as close to planlessness as we probably can get. The person dying of voodoo death after being hexed is almost planless. (The catatonic is inactive, but is executing a plan of being immobile.)

People may seek psychotherapy because their plans are no longer relevant or feasible. People may also find themselves with no plan. For example, (a) they may have brain damage, (b) the situation may be too complex or ambiguous for people to understand so that their planning mechanism turns off without producing a plan that can be executed, (c) they may be using borrowed plans (from parents or a boss), and the source of these plans is withdrawn, (d) they may have completed the execution of all of their plans, and they are ready to die, but do not do so, or (e) they are in a novel situation in which their old plans are not applicable.

If a person finds himself planless (especially suddenly), he will experience negative emotions. One possible reaction is to reinstate an old plan that is no longer relevant or feasible, and to continue to develop, transform, and execute it. Miller saw this as a paranoid reaction.

Alternatively, the person may keep as much of the strategy as possible and make revisions only in the tactics. The person may act out earlier situations, letting present persons symbolize earlier ones, a regression that Miller sees in schizophrenic reactions or depressions.

A third possibility is to give up the strategy, but keep the tactics. The survival of islands of involuntary plans may constitute obsessive-compulsive and hysterical neuroses and also catatonia. In these patterns of disturbance, habitual, ritualistic patterns of behavior substitute for the development of new useful plans.

Abandoning plans often or changing them often leads to anxiety. The patient may develop plans to deal with anxiety (such as the psychoanalytic defense mechanisms) instead of plans to cope with reality.

Individual Differences

People differ in their images. People differ in taste or ideas, words that refer to images. However, major differences also occur in plans, in the way they tackle problems and carry them through.

Plans of different people may differ in their source (whether a person uses his or her own plans or borrows those of others), in length of time the plans extend for, in whether plans are left as general strategies or have the tactics spelled out, in their flexibility (whether the order of execution of parts can be interchanged easily), and in other areas (for example, how rigid is the plan, how rapidly the plan was formed, how well the person coordinate several plans, how the person remembers details about the execution of the plan when it is operating, how open the person is about communicating the plans, and what kind of stop-orders the person builds into the plans).

Discussion

One problem with Kelly's concept of a construction system is that it is difficult to see how it leads to action. The concept of a plan as proposed by Miller and his associates overcomes this difficulty by making action a central feature of the concept. Lester (1987a) suggested a similar process to bring action into the picture. In a particular situation, people choose a specific goal, predict or imagine what will happen as they try to achieve their goal, and then test their predictions by acting in the situation. If the outcome is as expected, then all has gone according to plan. If the outcome is different from what was expected, then this feedback changes the process used for making the prediction, so that the people make a different prediction the next time. The process is, therefore, prediction, choice of tactic, action, and feedback.

JEAN PIAGET

Piaget (Flavell, 1963) distinguished between structures and functions in the mind. Functions remain invariant. They are biologically inherited modes of interacting with the environment and remain unchanged throughout our lives. The two basic functions are organization and adaptation.

All acts are organized, coordinated affairs, governed by laws. In adaptation, two processes (called *functional invariants*) exist. In *assimilation*, the mind utilizes something from the environment and incorporates it. The input is changed to fit the existing schemata in the mind (the particular structures existing at the time). However, some inputs cause changes in the schemata, i.e., *accommodation*. In most instances both processes occur simultaneously. An input is assimilated into an existing schema, but also causes changes in that schema, thereby causing the schema to accommodate. Behavior is most adaptive when assimilation and accommodation are in balance, but such perfect balances are rare and temporary. At the extremes, assimilation dominates in play, whereas accommodation dominates in imitation.

The structures of the mind are called *schemata*. Schemata form a framework into which incoming information can fit. Every pattern of input is compared with the existing schemata and assimilated, resulting in a modification of the schemata. The schemata serve to organize new knowledge. Piaget labeled schemata by the behavioral acts that they referred to, such as the schema of sucking or the schema of sight.

A schema is similar to a concept, category, or underlying strategy that subsumes a whole collection of distinct but similar behavior sequences. Schemata are cognitive structures and are fluid or plastic organizations to which other elements can be assimilated. The fact that schemata accommodate while assimilating attests to their dynamic and supple quality. Schemata extend their field of application so as to assimilate new and different objects, which Piaget called *generalizing assimilation*. Schemata also undergo internal differentiation, which Piaget called *recognitory assimilation*, so that one class of objects for example, may be reconceptualized into two distinct classes. The differentiation of a global schema into several new schemata provides a sharper, more discriminating perception of reality. Schemata can also group together to form complex and interlocking relationships with one another, which Piaget called *reciprocal assimilation*. Structures move toward a state of equilibrium. In an equilibrium state, the structure is clearly delineated, but typically there are inconsistencies and gaps in the schemata that eventually lead to their destruction. The process by which structures change from one state to another is called *equilibration*, and the result of the process is a new (temporary) state of equilibrium. Piaget, of course, was primarily interested in describing the stages of development that the child moves through, the so-called periods of development.

What motivates a person to engage in cognitive activities? Piaget postulated an intrinsic need for cognitive structures and, once they were generated, for perpetuating themselves through further functioning.

Flavell (1963) noted the congruence between Piaget's concepts and those of Kelly. Piaget's schemata are similar to Kelly's construction systems, and the processes of assimilation and accommodation are consistent with Kelly's theory.

CONCLUSIONS

When Kelly published his theory he made few references to the ideas and theories of others. However, we can see that others have had similar ideas both before and after Kelly's ideas appeared in print. Prescott Lecky in particular, appears to have thought along very similar lines to Kelly in his 1944 book. Lecky's definitions of terms such as *learning*, *psychological development*, and *anxiety*, for example, are almost identical to those proposed by Kelly in his 1955 book. Festinger's theory of cognitive dissonance is similar to Kelly' concept of hostility versus realistic acceptance of disconfirming evidence. Kelly's theory, however, is the most complete statement of these ideas and can be applied to many more situations than the more limited theories discussed in this chapter.

However, the theorists reviewed in this chapter have elaborated and extended some of areas of Kelly's theory, thereby increasing our understanding of the theory. For example, Festinger's theory generated a great deal of empirical research which is relevant to Kelly's notion of hostility. McReynolds used a concept of anxiety similar to that of Kelly's in order to suggest hypotheses about the experience of schizophrenics. Piaget has applied concepts similar to those of Kelly in order to understand the psychological development of children. And Lecky discussed such experiences as pleasure and love in much greater detail than did Kelly. Thus, although Kelly's theory is the most comprehensive cognitive theory of personality, these other theorists have suggested ways in which Kelly's theory can be extended and applied to even more phenomena than Kelly was able to consider.

III

HOLISTIC VIEWS

6

The Holistic Theory of Andras Angyal

The theory of personality proposed by Andras Angyal is rarely found in textbooks for theories of personality. However, Abraham Maslow, one of the founding scholars in the field of humanistic psychology and a theorist whom we have met in Chapter 3 and whom we will meet again in Chapter 7, held Andras Angyal in very high esteem, considering him the seminal holistic theorist. A holistic theory is one that first examines the mind as a whole, and then describes some of the parts, in contrast to an atomistic theory, which begins by examining the elements that make up the mind and then attempts to draw conclusions about the whole.

Angyal proposed a holistic theory in much greater detail than any other scholar has done. He outlined the problems and issues of a holistic perspective, and he proposed solutions to the problems. However, he kept his theory at an abstract level and rarely proposed specific content for the mind. Following chapters discuss how other, later theorists have made proposals about the actual content of the mind that nicely illustrate Angyal's concepts.

Angyal presented his ideas first in a book he wrote (Angyal, 1941). After his death, colleagues who valued his ideas edited his speeches and notes into a second volume (Angyal, 1965), and these two volumes contain the major statements of his theory.

WHAT IS A HOLISTIC THEORY?

The Gestalt psychologists of the 1930s, a group of German psychologists who came to America before the Second World War, noted that the whole is more than the sum of the parts. As an example of this principle, they described two lights, side by side, flashing on and off at different times. If the timing is just right, one sees movement—the light on the left appears to move to become the light on the right. There are merely two lights flashing on and off, but one perceives movement.

Many examples illustrate this point. Knowing the properties of oxygen and the properties of hydrogen will not help one predict the properties of hydrogen oxide, that is, water. We can look at piles of lumber, wallboard, roofing tiles, windows, and doors lying on a vacant lot, and yet have no conception of the form and feeling of the final house. In fact, hundreds of different styles of houses could be built with those same materials.

Angyal's first principle was that the personality is an organized whole and not a mere aggregate of discrete parts. You cannot understand the mind simply by studying its parts. Angyal used the term *whole* for the concrete organized

---

ANDRAS ANGYAL

Andras Angyal was born in a rural Transylvanian community in Hungary in 1902. He received a Ph.D. from the University of Vienna in Austria in 1927 and an M.D. from the University of Turin in 1932 (Hall & Lindzey, 1978; Hanfmann, 1968). His early research focused on perception and the systems of spatial coordinates used for orientation.

He emigrated to the United States in 1932 where he began as a Rockefeller Fellow in the Department of Anthropology at Yale University. There he participated in a seminar on the impact of culture on personality under the direction of Edward Sapir who became a close friend. He moved to Worcester State Hospital in Massachusetts, first as a psychiatrist in the research unit and then as director of research from 1937 to 1945. While there, Angyal conducted several psychological and physiological studies on schizophrenia and described a subtype of schizophrenia marked by bizarre somatic delusions. His book, *Foundations for a Science of Personality*, was published in 1941.

From 1945 until his death in 1960, Angyal was engaged in private practice in Boston, mostly working with neurotic patients. However, he lectured, consulted, and supervised students in several counseling centers, including those at Brandeis University and Harvard University. After his death, his colleagues at the Brandeis Counseling Center, Eugenia Hanfmann and Richard Jones, edited his unpublished papers, which appeared in 1965 as *Neurosis and Treatment: a Holistic Theory*.

---

object and the term *system* for the organization (or arrangement) of the whole. The *system principle* is the basis according to which the whole is organized. Every system has one and only one system principle.

Of course, the whole can be conceptually divided into parts, *subsystems*, each of which has a system principle, and subsystems can be conceptually divided into subsubsystems, and so on. Thus, there is a hierarchy, all the way down to the individual elements of the mind, i.e., wishes, thoughts, emotions, and behaviors. Maslow (1970) saw this hierarchy as as analogous to looking at an object through a microscope and gradually increasing the strength of the magnification. At the lowest level of magnification, we see the object as a whole. As we increase the level of magnification, we see several parts that make up the whole. As we increase the level of magnification, we see smaller and smaller parts until, perhaps, we can see the individual molecules or atoms that are the basis for the whole.

THE BIOSPHERE

The universe of life is called the *biosphere*. The biosphere includes the *individual* and the *environment*. In a holistic approach, the individual and environment are not really separate. They can be seen as different perspectives within the biosphere. The holistic approach has much in common with Asian philosophies, particularly Zen Buddhism. For example, Alan Watts (1961) suggested that nature doesn't push us around; neither do we push nature around. Rather we are both part of the pattern of life.

Let us take two simple examples. Perhaps you put this book down a while ago, and ate a piece of chocolate cake. You might have said, "I'm so hungry,

I could eat a horse," in which case you are attributing your eating of the cake to your own individual desire. Or you might have said, "That cake looked so delicious, I couldn't resist it," in which case you have attributed your eating of the cake to the environment, that is, the cake. Both are true, and both are distortions of the truth. The truth is that there was tension in the biosphere that was resolved by the cake moving from the table to your stomach. Like the Zen Buddhists, Angyal permitted us to use either the individual or the environmental perspective, but he wanted us to remember that each perspective is a distortion of the truth.

As a second example, consider the cake. It is on a plate on the table. Is it the environment? Yes. Now it is in your mouth, and you are chewing it. Is it the environment? Yes, I guess. Now it is in your stomach, and your digestive juices are changing its chemical structure. Is it you or the environment? Hmm. Now it is in your intestine, and the reconstituted molecules are being absorbed into your body. Is it you or the environment? You, surely. At some point, the cake changed, but the change was not sharp or abrupt. To label a particular point as the change-over point would be arbitrary.

In trying to formalize this, Angyal proposed that we could always view an event from these two perspectives, the self or the environment—or the *subject pole* and the *object pole*. He proposed a set of terms for the forces viewed from either perspective, terms which I do not particularly like, but which I present because I cannot improve upon them. For example, "interest" as a neutral term seems to me to have a subject pole connotation, and the terms "drive" and "craving" seem somewhat archaic for modern psychological theory. The following outlines the main points of his holistic view of the biosphere.

Object pole
Elements: relevance, valence, demand quality
Organized into:
  Axiomatic values
  Systems of values
  Environment's system priciple
Neutral terms
Elements: readiness to tension, tension, interest
Subject pole
Elements: attitude, drive, craving
Organized into:
  Axioms of behavior
  Systems of axioms
  Personal system principle

There are forces in the biosphere: drives from the subject (individual) pole and valences from the object (environment) pole. For example, "I am hungry," describes a personal drive; "The chocolate cake is irresistible," says that the cake has a valence. From the subject pole, an *attitude* is a readiness to behave in a particular way, and Angyal called the parallel property viewed from the object pole as a "relevance." For feelings, he suggested the words "craving" and "demand quality." But he also pointed out that we need neutral terms to express what is going on from a holistic perspective, and his suggestions were "tension," "readiness to tension" and "interest."

Note that this is what makes Angyal's theory better than others. Although he stresses a holistic viewpoint, he is prepared to consider the elements that make up the whole. Many holistic theorists will not make this step, and so their theories end at this point in the chapter. They have nothing further to say.

From the subject pole, the attitudes, drives, and craving are organized into *axioms of behavior*, *systems of axioms*, and finally, our *system principle*. From the object pole, the valences, relevances, and demand qualities are organized into *axiomatic values*, *systems of values*, and the *environment's system principle*.

This chapter will later discuss what our own system principle might be. What might the environment's system principle be? The most important part of the environment for us is the interpersonal environment and, in particular, the cultural environment. Compare living in a democratic society versus one run by a dictator who suppresses opposition. Or compare living in a Catholic-dominated society versus an Islamic-dominated society. These societies would be very different. The particular dichotomies I chose (democracy versus dictatorship or Catholic versus Islamic) may not be sufficient to label a system principle, but they clearly could play a part. The societies would be very different, and the people living in the societies would think, feel, and behave very differently.

SYSTEM PROPERTIES

Let us consider you for a moment. Your processes function to maintain life, and you are an *open system*. You assimilate new material—food at the physiological level and experience and information at the psychological level. You also produce. You mobilize energy, and create new physiological products (and wastes) and new behaviors and ideas. By drawing in foreign material, you grow at the expense of the environment.

Life could be defined as a process of self-expansion, and Angyal called this the *trend toward autonomy*. Human life consists of a trend toward increasing autonomy. This is a general direction with many expressions: curiosity, the desire to achieve, the wish to dominate, the need to defend one's integrity and maintain one's inviolacy, or the drive to acquire possessions. Angyal saw little point in making an inventory of all of these manifestations of the trend toward autonomy.

Angyal called the impact of the environment upon us *heteronomous forces*. Every event in the biosphere is a product of both of the these components: autonomous and heteronomous forces acting together to create an event. Some events have a stronger autonomous component, others a stronger heteronomous component, and still others a balance.

There may be setbacks in the trend toward increasing autonomy. Heteronomous forces may be so great as to counteract the autonomous trends, *passive setbacks*. Occasionally, the individual may make a strategic retreat in order to marshal forces to move forward again. But Angyal saw no evidence for a force leading to large-scale regressions, such as Freud's concept of a death instinct.

Angyal realized that his theory was still incomplete. People are not content with autonomous strivings. They seek to be part of a family, a group, a culture, and the universe, even to surrender themselves to this larger unit (a family or a culture) or to become one with God. These desires constitute the *trend toward homonomy*. Everyone has both trends, though one trend may be more obvious in one person as compared to others.

Remember that Freud's original version of psychoanalytic theory (see Chapter 2) proposed three types of desires—id, superego, and ego desires. However, homonomous desires do not fit well into any of those three types. If we were to add a fourth subset to Freud's classification of desires, I think homonomous desires would be a good candidate.

Either trend can become distorted and take over the personality. But typically both are always present, working side by side. Making love obviously involves sexual satisfaction, i.e., a manifestation of the autonomous trend. But it also involves joining together with another, being concerned with them, and communicating with them. This is a manifestation of the homonomous trend.

And so we have Angyal's system principle—the double trend toward autonomy and homonomy. Notice that this system principle is necessarily very abstract, very broad. It has to be in order to be valid for every single person who has ever lived or who will ever live.

Development for the individual involves the division, subdivision, and branching of the very general expression of the trends toward autonomy and homonomy into more and more specific attitudes, values, desires, and thoughts.

PERSONALITY AS A TIME GESTALT

The notion that personality is a *time gestalt* nicely summarizes Angyal's ideas. *Gestalt* is the German word for whole. The personality is always an integrated whole, which moves through time to realize the particular system principle of the individual. Thus, with age, there are fewer and fewer options, because the particular version of the system principle that the individual has chosen must be completed. In this sense, therefore, we become more rigid as we grow older.

Abraham Maslow, a few years before his retirement and death, told me that he had laid out a scholarly path for himself some 30 years earlier. He had wanted to accomplish particular goals and to explore particular topics from the humanistic perspective that he had developed. At the time we talked, he told me that he was working on the final paper he had planned those many years ago. He completed it, retired, and died soon after, a not uncommon occurrence (Weisman & Hackett, 1961; Lester, 1970). In his role as scholar, he had fashioned a particular form for his system principle, and he had wanted and needed to complete the plan.

The personality evolves over time, and there is continuity. Early events are not more important than later events (a proposition quite different from that of Freud); they are simply manifestations of the same theme. Mutilation anxiety in children is not the *origin* of later similar fears. It is merely the way in which a general fear, a threat to our safety and integrity, manifests itself in childhood. Later it may manifest itself as a fear that others are intruding into our space or that they are trying to tell us what we ought to think and feel or, in pathological states, that others can monitor our minds.

For Angyal, the past is not immutable, whereas Freud saw early traumatic events as having an inexorable effect on us. As an illustration of the Freudian notion of trauma, consider a tree with a nail knocked into it. The tree may continue to grow, and 50 years later, that rusted nail may be completely embedded deep inside the trunk of a healthy tree. The tree has dealt with the trauma of the nail and prospered. But it is, nevertheless, a tree with a scar deep within it, and it can never be the same as it would have been had the nail not been knocked into it.

For Angyal, on the other hand, the past is not immutable for it can be interpreted differently in the future. The significance of the past can change. The present can affect our interpretation of the past by merely reorganizing the parts of the pattern. If we correct an error in our computer program, then the new program runs efficiently, and there is no holdover (or "memory") from the period when it failed to run smoothly.

SYSTEMS AND INTEGRATION

Each item of behavior functions as part of several systems. Thus, each behavior has, or can have, many functions. *Plastic systems* are those in which the parts have variable functions. *Rigid systems* are those in which each part has a fixed function. A process in a rigid system is a localized happening, but a process in a plastic system can have an impact on neighboring parts. In a plastic system, an individual behavior may at one time be part of one system and, at another time, part of another system. This sharing of parts by different wholes is economical. At the physiological level, the processes of urination and sexual activity for males share some of the same anatomical structures. At the psychological level, consider a kiss. It can indicate friendship, sexual love, familial love, subordination (e.g., kissing the hand of a Pope), a person to be killed (e.g., Judas Iscariot's betrayal of Jesus), or simply respect (e.g., a European gentleman kissing a woman's hand).

As we develop, the parts become differentiated and reorganized. The different parts of the system become increasingly interrelated, and subparts differentiate from the parts that already exist.

Integration has to occur to keep the whole intact. In *vertical integration*, the specific behaviors you manifest must be tied to your particular expressions of the trends toward autonomy and homonomy. Typically the integration moves from the middle toward the depths and the surface. We know what we seem to have chosen to do. I am a professor and a writer. As I develop I become

---

THE CONCEPT OF INTEGRATION

Several theories of personality state that the psychologically healthy person is integrated, including the theories proposed by Carl Jung and Fritz Perls. What does the term *integration* mean? Lester (1987c) reviewed several ways in which the term is used.

In Angyal's theory of personality discussed in Chapter 6, we have two competing system principles, and each system principle has two component parts. Angyal's theory introduces two solutions. First, in the healthy person, the healthy system principle organizes the mind for more and more time. Thus, the goal is for the unhealthy system principle to be deprived of any executive power. One system principle eliminates the other. However, the healthy system principle has two components, the trends toward autonomy and homonomy, and the second goal is for these two parts to peacefully coexist. They must combine so that each behavior is, in part, an expression of both trends.

At the subsystem level, the goal of integration is often expressed as combining the material in the different subsystems into one organized whole. In Freud's psychoanalytic theory, for example, the goal of psychoanalysis is to move unconscious thoughts, desires, and emotions into consciousness. Thus, all of the psychological materials will move from being in two subsystems (the conscious and the unconscious) to being in one single system.

Other theories, however, see the subsystems as having impermeable boundaries, and combination of the different subsystems into one single whole would be a mistake. For example, it would not necessarily be a good idea to combine my different roles (as teacher, husband, son, father, scholarly colleague, and friend) all into one single role. There is merit in maintaining the roles separate. Integration in this perspective is harmony between the various subsystems, much like a smoothly functioning group of people or family.

---

more skilled in both tasks, that is, my surface behaviors become better suited to achieving my goals. But I also go though crises when I ask myself if this is what I *really* want to be doing. Do I want to be a professor? Are my day-to-day surface activities related to my deeper trends? Eventually, it would be good if there were a continuity between my deeper trends and my surface behaviors.

Progressive integration refers to the process by which we attain particular goals through particular means. Sometimes people fail to achieve goals, which suggests that they are using inappropriate means. I have a friend who *almost* has five graduate degrees. He did not pay the final fees necessary to receive his Master's in Education, is one course short of an M.S.W. and two courses short of an M.B.A., has completed 2 of the 3 years of law school, and did everything but the dissertation for a Ph.D. degree. He has a problem in his progressive dimension in this one area of his life!

Since we have several subsystems, and many subsubsystems, and so on, these parallel structures require *transverse integration*. These parallel structures must be coordinated (unless they are completely independent of one another, a situation that is unlikely except perhaps in disorders such as multiple personality).

Serious problems can occur with transverse integration. Particularly with plastic systems, it is important for the mind to be able to *set* and *shift set* easily and appropriately. For example, let us say that two of my subsystems are the role I have at work as a professor and my role at home as a husband. I have to be able to set in each role at the appropriate time. In class, I have to be organized as a professor and stay in that role. I have to *set* in the role. However, when I arrive home, I have to *shift set* and switch into my role as husband. If I stay in the role of professor, I may alienate my wife who may resent being treated like a student. (I remember my wife once asking me, during an argument, whether I would like a blackboard in order to explain my points more clearly!)

If subsystems are not allowed sufficient time for release, that is, sufficient time in control of the mind, symptoms occur. If one subsystem is much stronger than and dominates the other subsystem, the subordinate subsystem can only inhibit the dominant subsystem rather than share control of the mind. This leads to *symptoms of pressure* such as tenseness and nervousness.

As the subordinate subsystem gets stronger, it can sometimes interfere with the functioning of the dominant symptom, leading to *symptoms of intrusion* such as obsessions, compulsions, and excessive fantasy. As the subordinate subsystem gets even stronger, it can fight the dominant subsystem on equal terms and, if alternative sharing of control of some kind is not possible, then *symptoms of invasion*, may occur in which the person's behavior is chaotically controlled by two systems at the same time without coordination, leading to symptoms such as indecision, ambivalence, states of confusion, and catastrophic reactions.

Angyal did not consider the particular content of the mind or its subsystems. For example, he did not focus on the unconscious much at all. He did recognize that our conscious processes sometimes dominate the mind. He referred to this conscious part of our mind as our *symbolic self*, and he called unconscious processes *dynamic trends not symbolically elaborated*. However, because the content of the mind can be pathological (for example, in those who think delusionally or irrationally), the symptoms of pressure, intrusion, and invasion can lead to severely disturbed behavior.

DISTURBED BEHAVIOR

Angyal tried to maintain a holistic perspective when he considered disturbed behavior. His terms for health and disturbed behavior were *biopositive* and *bionegative*, but these adjectives referred to the *organization* of the mind, not to its contents.

Consider an apple. It looks good except for a part where it has been bruised. If we cut this bruised part out, then it will be fine to eat. This is *not* the conceptualization of the mind that Angyal adopted—healthy except for a small diseased part.

For Angyal, the mind is either completely healthy or completely disturbed depending upon the system principle organizing it. If the organizing system principle is a healthy one, then the mind is completely healthy; if the organizing principle is an unhealthy one, then the mind is completely disturbed. This all-or-none situation is reminiscent of George Kelly's bipolar constructs discussed in Chapter 3.

How then can an individual be a "little disturbed"? Angyal saw this as a matter of the relative amount of time for which the healthy and the unhealthy system principles were in control. In the healthy person, the healthy system principle organizes the mind for most of the time; in the disturbed person, the unhealthy system principle organizes the mind for most of the time.

Maslow (1942) once conducted a study of the sexual behavior of healthy and unhealthy women. He devised a psychological test to measure their psychological health and questioned them about their sexual history. He found that the psychologically healthy women were more likely to have engaged in all kinds of sexual behavior, including those that some in our society might consider perverted. Maslow reflected on this and concluded that there was not such a thing as a "perverted" behavior. There were, however, "perverted" people. However healthy people behaved, whatever they did was healthy because their minds were organized by a healthy system principle. In contrast, whatever a disturbed person did is unpleasant. The way in which such a person looks at you, shakes your hand, or eats food is unpleasant!

His students once asked Maslow whether a psychologically healthy person could murder another. Of course, he replied. It is the organization of the mind that determined the "goodness" or "badness" of the act. Killing for the correct reasons can be the act of a healthy person. Had one of Adolf Hitler's potential assassins succeeded in killing him, that person would have saved millions from death and been viewed as a hero of the 20th century.

Unhealthiness is, then, a way of life for Angyal. It is an organization with its own goals, attitudes, and motivations, and may lead to symptoms of pressure, intrusion, and invasion as it competes with the healthy way of life. Personality (or our mind) is, therefore, by necessity, a dual organization, each of the organizations governed by a different system principle—the *principle of universal ambiguity*.

The Gestalt psychologists of the 1930s used a visual analogy (see Figure 6.1). The picture there can be seen as a vase or as two faces. As the organization changes from one interpretation to the other, the parts of the picture do not move, but each part performs a different function. A more modern analogy is a computer (the mind) with alternative programs, for example, Microsoft Word as opposed to Lotus 1-2-3 (the system principles).

Each system defends itself against the rival system; the defense mechanisms are the tactics used by each system. The traditional psychoanalytic defense mechanisms (such as sublimation and projection) are ways in which the unhealthy system tries to prevent the healthy system from taking over control of the mind. Angyal pointed out that psychologists needed to define a set of defense mechanisms that the healthy system uses to prevent the unhealthy system from taking over. He suggested processes that he called *empathy*, *objectivity*, and *inventive thought*, terms that do not appeal to me. I think that defense mechanisms of the healthy system might be similar to strategies that psychotherapists use to help clients—strategies such as disputing irrational beliefs (which is used in cognitive therapy), uncovering the unconscious contributions to our behavior (which is used in psychoanalysis), and becoming more aware of our emotions (which is used in Gestalt therapy).

Figure 6.1   A reversible figure: a vase or two faces.

Angyal, like Freud, suggests that trauma early in life is the cause of the rival unhealthy system principle. Angyal considered only neurosis (although Chapter 7 discusses R. D. Laing's suggestion that Angyal's ideas can be extended easily to psychosis), and he proposed two patterns for the neurotic system principle.

The Pattern of Vicarious Living

The method of adjustment in the pattern of vicarious living is the systematic repression of one's genuine personality and an attempt to replace it with a substitute personality. This substitute personality has been called the *social self* or the *pseudo-self* by other writers, but I prefer the *façade self*, since it is the self we present to others and by means of which we seek to hide our real self. The strategy leads to symptoms such as feelings of emptiness and vacuousness, a pervasive dissatisfaction with the way we are, and attempts to escape from these feelings by getting signs of approval for our facade self from others.

Why should such a strategy be adopted? Angyal suggested that it was because the person felt unloved and unliked as a child. If children feel unloved by their parents, then they typically assume that it is their own fault. Therefore, in order to receive love and approval, they must suppress (and eventually repress) their real selves and become what they think others want them to be. Angyal noted that this was the pattern of disturbance proposed by almost all theorists, and we shall see in the following chapter that this seems to be the case.

This pattern leads to hysterical neurosis (now called *conversion disorder*), the hysterical and histrionic personality and, when negativism is present too, psychopathy (antisocial personality disorder).

THE BUDDHIST NOTION OF "NO-SELF"

Although we in the West are convinced that we have a "self," the Eastern philosophical system of Buddhism suggests that the self is an illusion (Kolm, 1985). For Westerners in general, the model of the mind is like a peach. If we remove the skin and the flesh of the peach, then we discover the peach pit. Similarly, if we removed the facade self that we show to others, and dismantle the defenses erected by the mind to protect us, we would discover at the center the "real self," the self we really are, but the self we show to only a few special others in our lives.

In contrast, Buddhists use the onion as an analogy for the mind. If we remove the outermost layer of the onion, we find another layer. If we remove that layer, we find yet another layer! And if we keep removing these layers, we are left with nothing, as onions have no pit, no seed, no core.

How then do we exist? Consider another Buddhist analogy, a river. There is water flowing through it, so that the river is never the same at one moment as it was in any other previous moment, because it never has the same molecules of water flowing in it. Yet the river exists; it has some permanence because the river bed, though it may shift over time, serves to channel the flowing water. A mind is like a riverbed in that it is a unique way of channeling sensory impressions. "A Buddhist observing you will see a pile of elements, a bag containing several hundred types of things, an aggregate of aggregates, a flux of events, a current of causal relations, but not *you*" (Kolm, 1985, p. 256).

The "self" is, therefore, a mental construction. If we could realize this, along with realizing that it is better to observe events rather than evaluate them and to avoid desiring things, then our suffering would be greatly reduced.

How then can we continue to exist if we must abandon the reality of the "self"? Alan Watts (1961) suggested that the game of life is to act *as if* there was a self, while knowing that that there really is not.

The Pattern of Noncommitment

This pattern results in a person who is confused as to whether the world is basically good and friendly versus bad and hostile. This leads to uncertainty and ambivalence. Are people good and trustworthy or bad and untrustworthy, and how can this confusion be dispelled?

These people express fear and hostility toward a presumably hostile world, seem confused and indecisive, and adopt techniques to dispel the confusion such as obsessions, compulsions, and rituals. If I do this in such a way, then today will be fine. I remember as a child that we believed that the day would go well if we managed to walk to school without stepping on the cracks in the sidewalk paving.

This pattern arises when children are faced with an inconsistent world. Today Daddy is kind and friendly, but yesterday he was angry. Yesterday, Mommy laughed at what we said, but today she hit us. Other people are unpredictable, and ambiguity comes to characterize every situation that the child faces. This pattern leads to anxiety and a search for ways to dispel the anxiety, frequently resulting in obsessive and compulsive behaviors and, in the extreme, obsessive-compulsive disorder.

Hysterics see the world as depriving them. Their desires remain unfulfilled. They see themselves as unliked and unlikable. Their goal is to gain approval.

Obsessive-compulsives see the world as threatening. If they are not careful, they may be destroyed. They feel weak and defenseless. Their aim is to develop skills to ward off enemies. Hysterics concentrate on the self. They feel empty and worthless. The obsessive-compulsive focuses on the environment, which is potentially threatening. Hysterics highlight the existential issue of life and death since they systematically "kill" (repress) their real selves; obsessive-compulsives highlight the existential issue of good and evil.

Eysenck (1967), coming from biological and learning perspectives, has also concluded that there are two types of neurotic patterns—hysteric neurosis/psychopathy and dysthymia (Eysenck's term for anxiety disorders).

DISCUSSION

Angyal's theory illustrates the problem of holistic theories. If we remain completely holistic, we are reduced to saying that each person is a completely unique individual. Period. To move beyond this, we have to stop being completely holistic. Angyal talks of subsystems and subsubsystems. He proposes a system principle, which really mandates two principles (one healthy and the other unhealthy), each of which has two components (the trends toward autonomy and homonomy and the patterns of vicarious living and noncommitment). What then makes Angyal holistic?

Angyal is holistic because he starts with the integrated whole and then breaks down the whole into parts. He does not go too far. For example, he rarely talks about individual desires, thoughts, or behaviors. Atomistic theorists, on the other hand, start with these elements (desires, thoughts, and behaviors) and try to build larger structures from them. The end result could be the same, but a comparison of Angyal's theory with those of Freud and Kelly already presented will reveal that the theories are very different. The concepts and, more importantly, the abstract perspectives that come from Angyal's theory are very different from those in Freud's and Kelly's theories.

Angyal's theory is not better than Freud's or Kelly's. Neither is it worse. It is different and, therefore, perhaps an ideal theory of personality ought to incorporate aspects of both atomistic and holistic perspectives because both have much to offer in helping to understand the human mind.

7

The Real Self and
the Facade Self

Andras Angyal felt that almost all theories of disturbed behavior proposed by other scholars focused on what he called the *pattern of vicarious living*. This chapter supports his assertion by reviewing some of the other theorists who have proposed a similar pattern. However, although the essence of these alternative versions of the pattern of vicarious living are similar to Angyal's version, they are often embedded in a different context that may change the connotations of the theory. Furthermore, they often use different terms, terms that some may prefer over those proposed by Angyal.

ARTHUR JANOV

Arthur Janov (1972), who developed primal scream therapy, has a theory of disturbed behavior that is in some respects similar to psychoanalytic theory. He felt that babies have important psychological and physiological needs that have to be gratified. These needs include being fed, held, stimulated, kept warm, and so forth. These needs are the *primal needs*. Babies often have their needs ignored because their parents fail to gratify them. Some babies suffer more frustration of their needs than do other babies. If their needs are consistently not gratified, babies learn to block out of their awareness (that is, repress) the emotions that accompany the deprivations. With continued severe deprivation, babies also learn to repress the needs themselves, and they will pursue substitute gratifications instead. Satisfying these substitute needs is seen by Janov as satisfying the primal needs symbolically. This is the essence of neurotic behavior—the symbolic satisfaction of primal needs. So far, Janov's theory resembles Freud's psychoanalytic theory quite closely.

Janov also focused on the demands that parents place upon their children— to get good grades, be quiet, be clean, and so forth. The greater the demands imposed upon the child by the parents, the more likely it is that the child's real needs will be unsatisfied. Each time this happens, the child experiences a *primal pain*, and the needs and their accompanying feelings are denied or repressed and become unconscious. These individual primal pains are added to the *primal pool*.

Typically, some event happens to the child that crystallizes all of these developments for the child, the *primal scene*. Some event takes place, and the child realizes that there is no hope of being loved for what he or she is. This major primal scene is of course merely one scene in a long sequence of scenes, but it is the one that is remembered and serves to symbolize the whole child-hood. The child learns to generalize from this one scene and make predictions about how the parents will behave thereafter. Janov felt that the primal scene, i.e., the one crucial for crystallizing the child's experience, usually occurs between the ages of 5 and 7.

After the primal scene, the child typically decides to repress all of the desires that are incompatible with the parents' goals. The child thereafter tries to please the parents in the way that the parents appear to want. The child suppresses the *real self* or *true self* and builds a shell around himself or herself, a defense system or *unreal self*. The real self and the unreal self then act in a constant dialectic contradiction, with the unreal self continually preventing the person's real needs from emerging and being fulfilled. This part of Janov's theory is very similar to the pattern of vicarious living described in Angyal's theory of personality.

Janov's theory has several holistic conceptions in it. For example, Janov saw symptoms as hooked into systems. Janov opposed treating only the symptoms of the patient. Rather, the therapist must treat the cause that *organizes* the symptoms. In fact, Janov noted that symptoms often do not disappear until quite late in the course of primal therapy, after the causes of the symptoms have been thoroughly explored. (Incidentally, Janov felt that symptoms are idiosyncratic solutions to the problem of satisfying the primal needs in a symbolic manner, and so there is no universal symbolism in the symptoms shown by patients.) The holistic aspects of Janov's views are manifest in his belief that "as long as any part of the unreal system is allowed to remain, it will stay vigorous and suppress the real system" (Janov, 1972, p. 413). A patient can not be merely a little neurotic, then. He is either healthy or neurotic, a conception also found in the theory of personality described by Andras Angyal. A person is not "just being neurotic; neurosis is his being" (Janov, 1972, p. 59).

For Janov, *fear* is the fear of not being loved. This fear threatens the child's existence and is repressed. *Anxiety* is the present arousal of this fear. Anxiety may or may not be conscious, but it is always rooted in the primal fear. It may be experienced, but it is rarely accurately focused. Fear relates to the past; anxiety to the present. *Tension* is the muscular concomitant of anxiety. Anxiety is the emotion; tension the movements that accompany it.

Janov divided feelings into genuine ones (those experienced by the true self) and pseudo-feelings (those experienced by the unreal self). Most common feelings, such as guilt, depression, rejection, shame, and pride are pseudo-feelings. For example, pride is experienced when the unreal self is successful.

> *Stripped of shame, guilt, rejection and all the other pseudo-feelings, he will understand that the pseudo-feelings are but synonyms for the covered great Primal feelings of being unloved. . . . The emptied-out neurotic will also learn how few are the feelings of man. (Janov, 1972, p. 74)*

Defenses are sets of behavior that automatically block primal (genuine) feelings. They can be involuntary (the typical psychoanalytic defense mechanisms) or voluntary (such as smoking, eating, or drug use). Defense mechanisms can also be classified as tension building (such as knotting your stomach muscles) or tension releasing (such as bed-wetting).

Janov used *neurosis* as a broad term, or rather he saw neurosis as underlying most of the minor psychiatric disturbances. In a broad sense, neurosis for Janov referred to the whole of the developmental mechanism described so far in this section. Neurosis indicates the ways that defense mechanisms are linked together. Neurosis can, therefore, result in all kinds of symptoms including the traditional neurotic symptoms as well as those of the personality disorders and the psychosomatic disorders.

Janov's theory can be reconceptualized as a mix of Freud's psychoanalytic theory and Angyal's holistic theory, and, in particular, Janov made what Angyal called the pattern of vicarious living the prototype of neurotic styles.

SIDNEY JOURARD

Sidney Jourard (1971a, 1971b) was concerned with one major issue in his writing, namely, what characteristics do psychologically healthy people have? He stressed a few characteristics of such people.

First, psychologically healthy people do not distort what they experience. They perceive it as it really is. If what they perceive is not in accord with their concepts, then they suspend their concepts. The willingness to suspend concepts and beliefs applies to one's self, to others, and to the world. There is also a willingness to inform and revise concepts with fresh inputs of perception. In contrast, the unhealthy person "chronically conceptualizes the world" and "freezes it in only one of its many possibilities."

This can easily be rephrased using the terms of George Kelly's personal construct theory. The healthy person is obviously building a more effective construct system and is the antithesis of hostile. The healthy person also is dilated rather than constricted. Jourard's view of health and Kelly's view are clearly congruent, at least in this respect.

A second important feature of healthy people is the willingness to disclose themselves, to permit others to know them as they now are. Their aim in disclosing themselves is to be perceived by other people as the person they know themselves to be. Healthy people are authentic. Jourard does qualify the conditions under which we actively disclose ourselves. Disclosure is appropriate when we feel it is safe to be known and when we feel that it will be beneficial to be known. (Jourard hints at the possibility that self-disclosure can be inappropriate and motivated by neurotic rather than healthy needs.)

Unhealthy people camouflage their true being, possibly to prevent criticism or rejection; this has the result that we are misunderstood by others. We join the "lonely crowd," and more importantly we tend to lose touch with our real selves. Jourard argued that "no man can come to know himself except as an outcome of disclosing himself to another person" (Jourard, 1971a, p. 6). Furthermore, self-disclosure encourages others to disclose themselves. There is reciprocity which, in turn, leads to intimacy.

DISCLOSING THE SELF

Meleshko & Alden (1993) took 84 female undergraduates, of whom 42 were classified as anxious by their responses to a test of social avoidance and distress whereas 42 were classified as non-anxious. Each participant then talked to a student posing as another subject in the experiment, the "confederate," who always began the conversation. The confederates disclosed only superficial and non-intimate information about themselves to some participants, but disclosed personal and highly intimate information about themselves to other participants.

How much did the 84 participants disclose about themselves to the confederate? The intimacy of the participants' disclosures was rated by the confederate and by another observer.

The non-anxious participants were more sensitive to the confederate than were the anxious participants. The non-anxious women disclosed less about themselves when the confederate was non-intimate than did the anxious women and more about themselves when the confederate was intimate than did the anxious women.

The mean ratings (on a scale of 1 to 7) of the intimacy of self-disclosure by the women were as follows:

anxious women—low intimacy confederate, 2.44
anxious women—intimate confederate, 3.61
non-anxious women—low intimacy confederate, 1.79
non-anxious women—intimate confederate, 4.39

Thus, the non-anxious women's level of self-disclosure was more appropriate to the confederate's level of self-disclosure than was the level of self-disclosure of the anxious women.

Pathology is a result, therefore, of less than optimal self-disclosure to others. Indeed it is often an *active* struggle to avoid becoming known by others. Neurotic and psychotic symptoms are "smoke screens interposed between the patient's real self and the gaze of the onlooker. . . . [They are] devices to avoid becoming known" (Jourard, 1971a, p. 32). Less than optimal self-disclosure leads, in Jourard's view to both physical, psychosomatic, and psychological illness.

Psychotherapy is seen by Jourard as involving catharsis, and additionally, self-disclosure and confession. By self-disclosure, patients begin to learn more about their authentic selves. Jourard sees the social system we live in, the social, political, and economic "facts of life," as requiring that we learn roles. Agencies of social control restrict what we reveal about ourselves to what is deemed sane, legal, and good. Society causes us to repress our authentic self, and this leads to illness. Jourard's view of the repression of our authentic self and its replacement by a socially defined role is identical to Angyal's description of the pattern of vicarious living.

A third component of Jourard's discussion of psychological health concerns the role of optimism versus pessimism, or as he calls it *inspiration* and *dispiration*. Dispiriting events are the fertile soil for illness; inspiring events for psychological health. Psychotherapy is seen by Jourard as an inspiring event.

Jourard's views are not sufficiently complex and well-articulated as to merit being called a theory. However, his views can be seen to be congruent with the theories of both Kelly and Angyal.

R. D. LAING

Angyal's pattern of vicarious living, reviewed in the previous chapter, was applied by Angyal only to neurotic patterns of behavior. This raises the question of whether it might also apply to psychotic patterns of behavior, or whether instead psychosis requires a different system principle. The ideas of R. D. Laing, a Scottish existential psychiatrist, suggest that the pattern of vicarious living may apply to psychosis and that, therefore, one unhealthy system principle will suffice.

The basic concept for Laing was *experience*, and Laing was concerned that people are not permitted by their parents, family, and society to have authentic experiences. What is the cause of this alienation from experience and this destruction of the self? Laing focused primarily upon the parents' behaviors toward the child, which he felt destroy most of the infant's potentialities. We are taught what to experience. We learn the right way to behave and the right way to feel. Laing (1969) sometimes used the term ego to refer to the false self that adjusts to an alienated and alienating social reality.

All people adopt a pseudo-self, a false outer self. All you can see of me is not the complete me, or perhaps not the real me. The schizophrenic feels a split between the mind and the body, and usually identifies the pseudo-self with the mind. Thus, the real self becomes disembodied. To be disembodied means that you have no sense of being biologically alive. Your body is but another object in the world. This disembodied self becomes hyperconscious, forms its own ideations and images, and develops a complex relationship with the body.

Because the schizophrenic has a disembodied real self, which is hidden behind the false self system, the real self is shut up, isolated, and impoverished. Ontological insecurity makes the real self fear engulfment by the identity of others, and it fears being destroyed by others. Thus, the schizophrenic's false self system is erected in order to protect the real self from attack. The schizophrenic does not gain any gratification from the activities of the false self. Hysteric people, in contrast, do gain much gratification from the actions of the false self, though they may deny this. Hysterics pretend that the gratifying activities are just pretense.

For the schizophrenic, the inner disembodied self hates and fears the false self. To assume an alien identity can be a threat to your own identity. People with catatonia try to strip themselves of all behavior in order to deal with this fear of take-over, and they fall into stupors. Schizophrenics, therefore, have adopted a false self system in order to protect their real self from our observation, but they are then threatened by the presence of the false self system they have erected. Their false self becomes a prison. The false self becomes more extensive, more autonomous, and more dead, unreal, false, and me-

A RESEARCH STUDY ON ONTOLOGICAL INSECURITY

Laing (1969) proposed that a psychologically healthy person has a secure sense of presence in the world as a real, alive, whole, temporally stable, and continuous person. This is ontological security. Those who have doubts about their existence experience ontological insecurity. For example, as a teenager, I used to wonder if I was not, perhaps, a character in someone else's dream and, when that person awoke, I would cease to exist. (A student in my course on theories of personality suggested that the times when this other person wakes up coincide with the times when I fall asleep.)

In order to explore this idea, a student and I devised a questionnaire to measure several aspects of these feelings: doubts about one's existence (e.g., I have occasionally wondered whether I really exist); the desire to be noticed by others, a component of the hysteric personality (e.g., I like being the center of attention); the desire to be remembered after death (e.g., It is important to me that my family name be carried on); and belief in the ability of the mind to separate from the body (e.g., Sometimes I have felt that my spirit or soul has left my body).

We presented our results in the form of a factor analysis that identifies clusters (factors) of variables that are associated (Table 7.1).

Table 7.1 Factor analysis of test scores

	Factor I	Factor II	Factor III
Mind/body separation	−0.10	0.23	0.87[a]
Living on in memory	0.35	−0.16	0.72a
Doubts about existence	0.04	0.83[a]	0.27
Desire to be noticed	0.83[a]	0.22	0.10
Neuroticism	0.09	0.81[a]	−0.14
Extroversion	0.84[a]	−0.05	0.04

[a]Variables have high factor loadings (i.e., are strongly associated with each other).

Scores on the subscale of "doubts about one's existence" were positively associated with scores on a measure of neuroticism. Thus, Laing's notion that ontological insecurity is central to psychological disturbance was supported.

In addition, scores on the subscale "desire to be noticed" were positively associated with scores on a measure of extroversion. It is commonly assumed that the hysterical personality is extroverted, and this result supported such an assumption.

Finally, scores on the subscales "desire to be remembered after death" and "belief in mind and body separation" were not associated with either neuroticism or extroversion.

chanical, while the real self also becomes impoverished, empty, dead, and more charged with fear and hatred because it is cut off from communication with the outer world.

Laing describes the inner self in the schizophrenic as follows:

1. *Its orientation is a primitive oral one, concerned with the dilemma of sustaining its aliveness, while being terrified to "take in" anything. It becomes parched with thirst and desolate.*

2. *It becomes charged with hatred of all that is there. The only way of destroying and of not destroying what is there may be to destroy oneself.*

3. *The attempt to kill the self may be undertaken intentionally. It is partly defensive (If I'm dead, I can't be killed); partly an attempt to endorse the crushing sense of guilt that oppresses the individual (who has no sense of a right to be alive).*
4. *The "inner" self itself becomes split and loses its own identity and integrity.*
5. *It loses its own realness and direct access to realness outside itself.*
6. *The place of safety of the self becomes a prison. Its would-be haven becomes a hell. It ceases even to have the safety of a solitary cell. Its own enclave becomes a torture chamber. The inner self is persecuted within this chamber by split concretized parts of itself or by its own phantoms that have become uncontrollable. (Laing, 1969, pp. 172–173)*

The false self system and the inner self can also split into fragments, which leads to chaotic nonentity. This molecular splitting, even of the sequence of behavior, is common to schizophrenics (whereas, in the hysteric, the splitting is molar—that is, occurs between subsystems). In occasional cases of psychosis, Laing notes that what appears to have happened is that the false self system has been suddenly stripped away, revealing the ontologically insecure and disembodied inner self.

Laing, like Angyal, described a particular form of psychopathology involving the split between the real inner self and the false self system, much as in Angyal's description of the pattern of vicarious living. Laing added a more complex description of the types of false self systems and real (inner) selves that can arise, in particular, differentiating between those found in the hysteric and those found in the schizophrenic individual. Thus, although Angyal saw the pattern of vicarious living as part of the neurotic system principle, Laing's theorizing suggests that the same pattern can used to explain and describe what is going on in the psychotic individual, which represents an important step forward in our understanding of human behavior, both normal and abnormal. Note also that this description of schizophrenia is quite different from that provided by George Kelly's theory of personal constructs (see Chapter 4) and McReynold's perceptualization theory (see Chapter 5).

CARL ROGERS

In addition to describing a technique for conducting psychotherapy (called among other things *Rogerian therapy, nondirective therapy*, and, most recently, *person-centered therapy*), Carl Rogers has also described a theory of personality. The most explicit formulation of this theory is found in Rogers (1959).

Rogers suggested that the infant has an inherent tendency toward actualizing its organism, and its behavior is directed toward satisfying this need. If this need is satisfied, the infant experiences pleasure. Rogers noted that the infant is best conceptualized as an organized whole or as a gestalt. Furthermore, *the infant's perception* of the environment is more critical in affecting its behavior than the environment "as it really is."

SELF–IDEAL SELF DISCREPANCY

Scott & O'Hara (1993) examined the self–ideal self discrepancy in anxious and depressed university students to explore its importance in explaining psychopathology

They gave participants in the study a questionnaire in which they were asked to list up to 10 words to describe the folowing:

1. The attributes they actually posses—the self
2. The attributes they would ideally like to possess—the ideal self
3. The attributes they believed their parents would like them to possess—the ought self— a measure that is relevant to Rogers' concept of the conditions of worth imposed by parents upon their children.

The lists of attributes for each participant were compared with a computerized thesaurus to identify synonyms and antonyms, and these were used to generate discrepancy scores.

The university students were classified as meeting clinical criteria for major depression or dysthymia (the depressed group), for an anxiety disorder, for both, or for neither.

As expected, the depressed and depressed/anxious participants had significantly higher self–ideal self discrepancy scores than the normal participants. (The anxious participants obtained moderate scores.) However, the anxious participants did not differ from the depressed, depressed/anxious, and normal participants in their self–ought self discrepancy scores.

Scott and O'Hara concluded that clinical depression was associated with higher self–ideal self discrepancies, but they were not able to conclude that clinical anxiety was associated with higher self–ought self discrepancies.

Part of the process of actualizing involves differentiation, and soon a portion of the child's experience becomes symbolized in an awareness of being. This awareness may be described, according to Rogers, as self-experience. Eventually, this awareness becomes elaborated into a concept of self.

About this time of development, the child develops a need for positive regard. This need is universal, pervasive, and persistent. Rogers does not have an opinion as to whether the need is innate or learned. When the child interacts with adults, particularly his mother, it begins to search for and be satisfied by love from her. The likelihood of receiving this maternal love eventually becomes more important in determining its behavior than its need to actualize itself.

Soon the child develops a need for positive self-regard, and whether the child feels this positive self-regard will depend to a large extent on whether its parents give it positive regard. Typically, parents set up conditions of worth, that is, they regard the child positively only if certain conditions are met. Their regard for it is said to be conditional. As a result, such a child will have positive self-regard only if it meets these conditions of worth.

In contrast, in the healthiest environment, a child would receive unconditional positive regard. The child would be prized and valued by its parents no matter what it is or what it does. In this case no conditions of worth would be set up. Rogers felt that this case was hypothetically possible and theoretically important but not found in the actual world.

Once conditions of worth are set up, then the child begins to experience discrepancies between the conditions of worth and its actual experiences. When experiences are in accord with its conditions of worth, Rogers felt that the child will accurately perceive and symbolize the experiences. When the experiences are not in accord with the conditions of worth, the child's perception of the experiences may be selective and distorted. (Note that this resembles George Kelly's concept of hostility discussed in Chapter 4.) This process tends to break down the unity of the organism. Certain experiences tend to threaten the child's self. To maintain his or her self-concept, the child has to resort to defensive maneuvers. The child's behavior is regulated sometimes by his or her self and sometimes by elements of experience that are not included in the self. The personality becomes divided. The self is no longer true to itself. For the sake of preserving the positive regard of others, the self has falsified some of the values it has experienced. Rogers notes that this is not a conscious choice, but a result of the child's development in the presence of his or her parents.

The incongruence between the child's self and its experience leads to incongruencies in its behavior, some of which are consistent with his or her self and some with experiences that have not been assimilated into its self. Experiences that are incongruent with the self and with the conditions of worth are *subceived* as threatening, by which Rogers implied that the perception of threat is not necessarily conscious. The nature of threat is that, were the experience to be perceived accurately, then the conditions of worth would be violated. Then the need for positive self-regard would be frustrated, and the child would feel anxiety.

This leads to neurosis. Neurosis basically involves selectively perceiving—denying to awareness some aspects of your experience and distorting your experience in order to keep your total perception of experience consistent with your conditions of worth. Rogers includes in such maneuvers psychological processes such as rationalization, compensation, fantasy, projection, compulsions, phobias, paranoid behaviors, and catatonic states.

If the incongruence between an experience and the conditions of worth is large, occurs suddenly, and has a high degree of obviousness, then these neurotic defensive coping mechanisms cannot operate successfully. Anxiety will be experienced and a state of disorganization will exist. We would see such an individual undergo an acute psychotic breakdown. The person's behavior will appear to be irrational. Typically, the behavior is consistent with the denied aspects of experience rather than consistent with the self. For example, if people have kept their sexual impulses under rigid control, denying them as an aspect of their self, then during their state of disorganization they may act upon such sexual impulses.

An individual undergoing such a process may take one of two paths. The denied experiences may stay dominant and the person will defend against an awareness of the self. Alternatively, the self may regain dominance, but it will be a greatly altered self. For example, the self will probably contain the theme that the self is a crazy, unreliable person with no control over its impulses.

Clearly, Rogers has provided a detailed analysis of the pattern of vicarious living as described by Angyal. Rogers has adopted a holistic viewpoint, and he has described the process by which the pattern of vicarious living develops. Rogers has added, however, a detailed examination of this process that clarifies it greatly, and he has added some suggestions as to how psychosis might be incorporated into the framework, something that Angyal did not attempt to do. Over the years, Rogers' terminology has become very popular and is the most commonly used way of describing the pattern of vicarious living.

EDWIN WAGNER

Edwin Wagner (1971) has proposed a distinction in personality that is similar to the ideas reviewed already in this chapter. Wagner has argued that personality can be seen as the result of two psychological structures: a *facade self* and an *introspective self*.

The facade self is a hierarchically organized set of attitudes and behavioral tendencies that are acquired early in life and that become automatic. These tendencies constitute our basic contact with reality and are formed at a preverbal level. These tendencies include our perception and automatic reactions to stimuli. The facade self is environmentally programmed (that is, determined by the environment).

The introspective self includes our conscience, motivation, and perseverance and has an evaluative and corrective effect on the facade self. The introspective self develops later in life as we become more cognizant of our behavior and as we establish a self-concept. Our introspective self includes such entities as our fantasies, our ideals, and our life-styles. It is heavily dependent upon our language and verbal processes. The introspective self has an enlarged sense of identity, which derived initially from our awareness of the operation of the facade self and subsequently expanded to include moral judgments, personal aspirations, life-style, conscience, and general philosophical outlook. It is internally programmed (that is, self-generated).

The facade self leads to reactions with little reflection or premeditation. It is focused upon the specific and concrete here and now. It is analytic. The introspective self does not lead to behavior directly (except for fantasy, talking to oneself, and rumination). It leads to behavior only by acting upon the facade self. The introspective self deals with wishes, possibilities, and potentialities. It is synthetic and tends to condense, simplify, and organize.

The facade self and the introspective self are structurally distinct, according to Wagner, but functionally interrelated. The direction of influence is from the introspective self to the facade self. The facade self tries to preserve itself as it is by means of coping mechanisms, which are analogous to psychoanalytic defense mechanisms. The most efficient coping mechanisms are intellectualization, routine activities (becoming compulsively preoccupied with environmental activities), socialization (joining groups such as a church or a club), professionalization (identifying with your work), and sexualization (providing proof of one's masculinity or femininity through one's clothes, activities, or attitudes). The less efficient coping mechanisms are repression, dissociation, and denial.

The distinction between these two "selves" is quite similar to that made by Rogers in his distinction between a person's introjected conditions of worth and his or her experiences, or Jourard's authentic self and social self. However, the particular phrasing that Wagner uses leads to different implications. For example, the introspective self develops later in life. It is not that the healthy child is made unhealthy by the behavior of its parents and represses its true identity. The introspective self involves a cognitive appraisal that is possible only with maturity. In addition, Wagner has applied his structural analysis to a variety of psychopathological types in a much more complex way than other theorists. Let me give some examples.

The facade self and the introspective self complement each other and reciprocate, but they may conflict. If the introspective self is extensive and strong and the facade self is weak, the result may be paranoid and schizoid types who are richly endowed with fantasy, delusions, and idiosyncratic thinking. The facade self is necessary for reality-oriented behavior. The delusions and disturbed cognitions in the schizoid patient come from the introspective self. Wagner noted that, in the paranoid patient, these cognitions are oversimplifications.

Other variants of schizoid patients exist. In one type, the introspective self is weak and the rigid facade self is held together by strong intellectualization. In another type, the facade self is not weak so much as warped. The patient clings to his or her inappropriate behavioral repertoire and refuses to change it (thereby behaving rigidly), or else escapes into the fantasy of his or her introspective self.

Why should the facade self be weak? Perhaps the child's early experience was so traumatic that learning is impaired? Or perhaps the child has neurological damage that impairs learning.

If both the facade self and the introspective self are well developed but in conflict, then symptoms of neurosis will occur. Wagner discussed various kinds of structural possibilities that lead to neurotic symptoms.

1. A simple conflict exists between the facade self and the introspective self.
2. Discrepancies exist between the facade self, the introspective self and the environment. As a result the patient engages in self-deprecatory ruminations (leading to anxiety) or blames others (leading to anger and hostility).
3. In conversion hysteria, the introspective self is underdeveloped, and the patient tries to deal with the environment with a rigid facade self. Alien impulses (particularly sexual and aggressive ones) are prevented from having any behavioral expression. The rigid facade self is weak, immature, and passive, but socially appropriate. The facade self is disconnected from emotional reactivity, that is to say, an event can elicit an emotional response viscerally speaking but is denied awareness and behavioral expression. The facade self does not permit alien impulses (particularly sexual and aggressive impulses) from having any behavioral expression. Insight is poor, because the introspective self is underdevel-

oped and because the facade self does not permit the expression of
certain tendencies or impulses.

4. In the dissociative neuroses, the facade self is similar to that of the hysterical
neurotic, but the introspective self is more developed. However, the introspective self is not well integrated with the facade self and so is not readily
manifest in the patient's behavior.

In both the hysteric neurotic and the dissociative neurotic, the facade self
is rigid, pseudosocialized, weak, and immature. But it is socially appropriate. The facade self is disconnected from visceral reactivity, so that visceral
responses occur, but they are denied awareness and behavioral expression.
Wagner emphasizes that a rigid facade self is inimical to the expression of
impulses.

In conversion hysteria, stimuli from the environment create a visceral
response, but they fail to have a cognitive response due to the impaired
introspective self. The inner turmoil is neutralized through the development
of physical incapacities. The weakness of the introspective self precludes
fantasy outlets and cognitive outlets for the visceral emotional responses.
The facade self does not permit behavioral expression of the emotional
responses, or rather, does not have a behavioral repertoire that includes
action tendencies that are capable of expressing the forbidden wish.

5. The psychopath, who has a character disorder, has a functioning facade self
and a weak introspective self. What differentiates him from other character
disorders and from the hysteric neurotic is that his facade self has a veneer
of social skills that facilitates the manipulation of others without the in-
vestment of any genuine emotion (positive or negative). The psychopath is
not necessarily aggressive, criminal, or sexually disturbed. Since his introspective self is weak, he has a poor self-concept, is poor at long-range
planning, and is deficient in responsibility, fantasy and imagination, and
individuality. His primitive emotional needs, although weak, demand immediate gratification without regard for others, and his facade self has the
behavioral repertoire necessary for such gratification.

It can be seen that Wagner makes use of one other concept other than the
strength of the facade and introspective selves, namely that of their content.
Is the facade self rigid? Does it possess a behavioral repertoire to permit
manipulation or the expression of emotions? Does the introspective self deal
cognitively with emotions?

Wagner's views are similar to Angyal's discussion of the neurotic pattern of
vicarious living (the hysteric neurotic), and note that Wagner uses his theory
most extensively to describe the hysteric neurotic and the psychopath, both of
whom Angyal classifies in the pattern of vicarious living. However, Wagner is
also able to successfully describe other disorders, and in particular schizophrenic psychoses.

DISCUSSION

This chapter has reviewed the theories of five personality theorists who have
analyzed the concepts of the real self and the facade self. Each uses different

terms for this distinction, and each embeds the terms in a theory that has unique connotations and implications. Some of these conceptualizations are more well known than others, and the reader may prefer one over the others. However, Angyal seems on the whole correct in asserting that the pattern of vicarious living has been a common proposal from personality theorists over the years.

8

Concept of Subselves

Many of the major theorists of personality have proposed that the mind is made up of many subselves. For example, Eric Berne (1961) talked of *ego states*; Carl Jung (Progoff, 1973), of *complexes*; Abraham Maslow (1970), of *syndromes*; Gordon Allport (1961), of *traits*; Henry Murray (1959), of *themata*; and Andras Angyal (1965), of *subsystems*. Each of these terms refers to holistic, complex, and organized component parts of the personality, what we may call *subselves*. This chapter reviews the theories of those who have developed this idea.

As discussed in Chapter 6, Angyal presented his theory in very abstract terms. He gave very few concrete examples of his concepts, and I was not able to give as many illustrations as I did, for example, when introducing Freudian concepts in Chapter 2. Two theorists who have independently provided concrete examples that fit nicely into Angyal's abstract schema are Carl Jung and Eric Berne. As their theories complement Angyal's theory, I will describe these two theories first.

CARL JUNG

Jung's term for the totality of psychological processes was the *psyche*. Jung proposed that *complexes* exist within the psyche, autonomous partial systems that are organizations of psychic contents. Complexes are subsystems of the whole. (The complexes in the collective unconscious are identical to the archetypes.) In particular, Jung identified several complexes that he felt were of particular use for a discussion of human behavior.

The ego consists of our conscious psychic contents and contains percepts, memories, thoughts, desires, and feelings. The persona is a subsystem within the ego and is the self that we present to others, the mask we wear in daily intercourse with others. It consists of the roles we play in our lives. Because we have several roles, it makes sense to speak of various components of the persona.

The *shadow* consists of those psychic contents in the personal (and to a lesser extent the collective) unconscious that are in opposition to the contents of the ego. These contents are less developed and less differentiated than the contents of the ego, but their presence is made apparent to the ego whenever the boundaries between the systems break down and contents from the shadow intrude into the ego.

In addition, the subsystem in the collective unconscious that is in opposition to the persona subsystem of the ego is called the *anima* in males and the *animus* in females. By modern standards, Jung erred here in identifying the core of human behavior in terms of the social sexual stereotypes of his day. Jung described males as "masculine" and females as "feminine," in what today would be considered a gender-biased fashion. For example, Jung described the unconscious animus of females as rational and discriminating, showing that Jung believed females to have inevitably an irrational and emotional conscious ego. Today, we have no need to accept all of Jung's ideas wholesale. We can better conceptualize the anima and animus as the subsystems of the shadow that are in opposition to the persona and that permit their content to vary depending upon the psychic contents of the particular persona. (Perhaps we could call these both "animum," using the Latin neuter gender?)

The self is the part of the psyche that eventually becomes the synthesized whole. The self represents the combination of the opposed parts of the psyche organized into a unified whole.

Psychic Functions and Attitudes

Jung suggested that the psyche responds to stimuli (internally or externally generated) by sensing them, interpreting them, evaluating them, and sometimes having an immediate awareness of them. He called these functions *sensation, intuition, thinking,* and *feeling.* He suggested that these functions are developed to differing degrees within each person, thereby providing a basis for categorizing people. Jung conceptualized these functions in pairs: sensing versus intuition, thinking versus feeling. The ego typically develops one of these functions more fully than others, and the opposite function of the pair becomes the strongest function of the shadow.

Jung also distinguished two attitudes of the psyche. The attitude of extroversion orients the person toward external stimuli; the attitude of introversion orients the person toward internal stimuli. If the conscious part of the psyche (the ego) adopts one attitude, then the personal unconscious (the shadow) will have the other attitude.

Abnormal Behavior

Abnormal behavior can result from various causes in the psyche. The goal of the psyche is to unite into a complete whole, a process called *individuation.* Perhaps in order to unite, the psyche has to fragment into various subsystems first. Abnormal behavior can result from one subsystem becoming dominant over another or from one subsystem taking over the system of which it is but a part. For example, in some people the persona takes over the ego. The person who was presenting himself as a teacher initially now becomes a Teacher. Other aspects of his ego are suppressed by the persona.

Neurosis for Jung was a term to describe the condition in which a group of psychic contents (a complex) moves from the unconscious and disturbs the conscious. It occurs whenever any particular system or subsystem (or complex) has become overdifferentiated from the others. The goal of the unconscious is to restore the balance in the psyche whenever the conscious psychic contents

---

RESEARCH ON JUNG'S TYPES

Jung defines two attitudes (extroversion versus introversion) and four functions (sensing versus intuiting and thinking versus feeling), which he felt characterized people, and Myers & Briggs (1987) devised a psychological self-report inventory to measure these three pairs of traits, adding a fourth pair that they labeled perceiving versus judging. This psychological test has stimulated a great deal of research.

Jenkins, Stephens, Chew, & Downs (1992) explored whether scores on the Myers-Briggs Type Indicator, as the test is called, predict empathic responding in counselors. Empathy is a counseling skill in Carl Roger's person-centered therapy in which the counselor responds to and enhances the words and emotions expressed by a client. A group of graduate students ($N = 56$) enrolled in a course on counseling theory were given the Myers-Briggs Type Indicator. After watching a film of clients with different personal problems, the students wrote therapeutic responses that were rated for the level of empathy. The correlations between the level of empathy and the personality test scores are as follows.

extroversion–introversion	.05
judging–perception	−.10
sensing–intuition	.14
thinking–feeling	.46

Only scores on the thinking–feeling scale predicted empathic responding (i.e., were statistically significant at the 5% level or better), with those counselors receiving higher feeling scores responding more empathetically. In addition, gender (female) and high grade-point averages predicted higher levels of empathy. These three variables together accounted for 46% of the variance in empathy scores.

---

begin to dominate the psyche. The more the conscious systems become autonomous, the more the unconscious systems will become autonomous, leading to an inner cleavage in the psyche. Thus, a neurosis is a state of being at war with oneself, a dissociation of personality. To cure a neurosis, the contending systems (and their system principles) must be fused into a new entity, greater than either alone (that will then be the "self"). The integration of the psyche, therefore, requires that it split first.

If a person grows up in a society that contains conflicting values and ideas, this dissociation of the psyche is facilitated. If, on the other hand, a person identifies with an established belief system in the society, then neurosis is less likely.

A psychosis is differentiated from a neurosis only by the degree of control exerted by the conscious part of the psyche over the unconscious complexes. In a psychotic person, elements of the unconscious intrude into the conscious ego. If the intrusion is partial, the ego may merely continue to exist with this unassimilated element. If the intrusive element is integrated into the ego, the ego may identify with it and accept it as an ego-derived element. Perhaps a psychotic who hears a voice has an unassimilated element deriving from the unconscious; one who has a delusion has identified with an autonomous (partial) complex from the unconscious. In a neurotic, the conscious elements of the ego remain in control of the psyche; in a psychotic, the unconscious elements are in control.

The neurotic will have symptoms that stress their weakest activity. For example, if the ego has most fully developed the thinking function, the neurotic will have symptoms involving feeling activities. The symptom therefore describes what the ego is not doing; it establishes an agenda and points to the direction that the psyche must take.

The infant's psyche is undifferentiated and whole. Maturation and growth lead to differentiation and splitting of psyche contents. Psychological health involves synthesis of the separate parts. The basic goal of the psyche then is integration, or *individuation*. Individuation involves the balancing and harmonizing of the psyche. Jung's concepts typically involve opposed systems, processes, functions, and attitudes, and so synthesis of these opposites makes an obvious end state for the psyche to attain. This feature of Jung's ideas is sometimes called "the principle of opposites." The majority of the "splits" in the psyche that Jung considered involve splits between conscious elements or complexes and unconscious elements or complexes. The splits could, of course, be between conscious elements or, alternatively, between unconscious elements, but such splits were not considered as important.

Discussion

This presentation of the structural elements of Jung's theory show that it closely resembles the theory proposed by Angyal. Both Jung and Angyal are concerned with systems within the personality. Both feel that synthesis and unification of the personality are the goal of the individual. For Jung, the basic goal of the psyche is integration, or individuation; for Angyal, the personality moves toward completing the gestalt that represents the meaning of the personality. Jung describes problems of psychopathology in terms of complexes splitting off autonomously, growing too large at the expense of one another, and intruding into and invading one another; Angyal proposes a similar basis for psychopathology.

Jung and Angyal differ in their focus of interest. Whereas Angyal was interested in the system principle of the personality, that is, the long-range goals of the personality vis à vis the environment, Jung was much more interested in the nature of particular complexes, such as the shadow and the persona, and in the kinds of complexes or archetypes found in the collective unconscious. Angyal's theory remains much more of an abstract set of concepts and principles, whereas Jung was more concerned with the specific contents of the psyche of each person. Thus, Jung provides a rich set of ideas for the content of Angyal's abstract theory.

One other point of great importance in Jung's theory is that he introduced a new idea that is not contained in the three fundamental theories with which I introduced this volume (the theories of Freud, Kelly, and Angyal). Jung's notion that, for each system in the ego, a complementary system must exist in the shadow is not found in any other psychological theorist. Indeed, the only other place in which I have found this idea is in the writings of the Kenneth Boulding (1968), an economist whose ideas are considered later in this chapter. Although we have read, and will read, other ways of presenting the ideas of

Freud, Kelly, and Angyal, and occasionally some elaborations of and alternatives to their ideas, only Jung's theory introduces a new principle.

ERIC BERNE

Berne (1961, 1964) proposed three new theories: a theory of personality, a theory of interpersonal relationships, and a system of psychotherapy. This section only discusses his theory of personality, which he has called *structural analysis*.

Berne built upon the ideas of Paul Federn (1952) and Edoardo Weiss (1950). Whereas psychoanalytic theory usually uses the terms *id, ego,* and *superego* to characterize particular wishes, Berne followed Federn and Weiss in defining ego states. An *ego state* is a coherent system of feelings and behavior patterns. Complete ego states can be retained in the memory permanently. The defense mechanisms can operate upon complete ego states and, for example, ego states can be repressed as a whole. Ego states from earlier years remain preserved in a latent state, with the potential to be recathected.

Structural analysis is concerned with analysis of ego states. Berne classified the psychological processes of the person into three parts. He gave them three useful labels, invented three "organs" that govern them, and three definitions.

Parent (exteropsyche)—identifying ego state
Adult (neopsyche)—data processing ego state
Child (archeopsyche)—regressive ego state

The Parent ego state is a judgmental ego state, but in an imitative way (primarily, of course, by imitating the person's parental judgments). It seeks to enforce borrowed standards. The Parent ego state parallels the superego in psychoanalytic theory. The Adult ego state is concerned with transforming stimuli into information and processing that information. It corresponds to the ego in psychoanalytic theory. The Child ego state reacts impulsively, using prelogical thinking and poorly differentiated and distorted perception. It corresponds to the id in psychoanalytic theory. However, although this simple correspondence is worth mentioning, the id, ego, and superego are *sets of wishes*, while the Child, Adult, and Parent are integrated and coherent *ego states*. Berne felt that his three basic conceptual units should be distinguished carefully from the psychoanalytic terms of superego, ego, and id. For example, the Child ego state has an organization, a unified will, logical processes, and negation, which make it very different from the psychoanalytic conception of the id.

People are always in some ego state. They can shift from one to another and these ego states are usually Parent, Adult, or Child ego states. When people shift from one ego state being predominant to another being predominant, Berne talks of psychic energy flowing from one state to another, a concept in the theory that is unnecessary for modern theories of the mind. The state that is predominant is said to be *cathected*. (Note that the terms

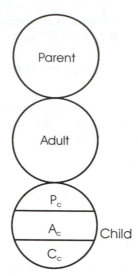

Figure 8.1   Structural analysis of the Child.

cathect and cathexis are used differently in Berne's theory than in Freud's theory—see Chapter 2.) It has executive power for the moment and is experienced as the real self. Berne also talks of cathexis flowing from one state to another, again in a similar manner as psychoanalytic theory. The use of the terms *energy* and *cathexis* seems old-fashioned today. Angyal's terms *set* and *shifting set* describe the processes involved in a more current way and fit better with modern psychological theory.

Each ego state is an entity in Berne's theory, which is differentiated from the rest of the psychic contents. It has a boundary that separates it from other ego states. However, the ego boundaries are semipermeable under most conditions. The shift from one ego state to another depends on the forces acting on each ego state, the permeability of the boundaries of each ego state, and the capacity of each ego state to be cathected.

Ego states can affect behavior directly by being the predominant ego state of the moment, or by influencing other ego states (c.f., the discussion of Angyal's symptoms of pressure in Chapter 6). The primary ego state that Berne talks of as having an influence is the Parent. For example, the Child can function as an independent state (free) or under the Parent's influence (adapted).

The analysis of ego states can be made much more complex. A small child has three ego states: a Parent ego state, and Adult ego state, and a Child ego state. When a trauma occurs that fixes these ego states, all three are fixed. Thus a particular Child ego state that an adult has, in fact, has three components: a primitive Child ego state, a primitive Adult ego state, and a primitive Parent ego state. Similarly, this primitive Child can be subdivided into three ego states (Parent, Adult, and Child), and so on. The Child ego state of an adult therefore has many components (Figure 8.1.).

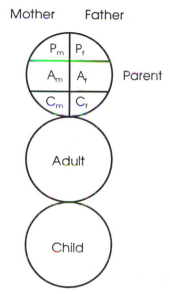

Figure 8.2   Structural analysis of the Parent.

The Parent ego state is an introjection of our parents' demands. But we had two parents. Therefore, our Parent ego state is a dual ego state (Figure 8.2). Secondly, our parents had three ego states, as well as parents (our grandparents) and so on.

Such an analysis could, in theory, go all the way back to Adam and Eve, giving us a truly collective unconscious, since our Parent ego states will have common components, transmitted from our common ancestors by introjection of ego state components.

Berne also speculated that the Adult ego state was composed of several components. Adult ego states have an openness that is childlike. He called this *pathos*. The Adult ego state also possesses qualities such as sincerity and courage, which Berne called *ethos*. The Adult ego state therefore has childlike and parent-like qualities, not due to any influence from the Child and Parent ego states, but on its own. The Adult ego state may therefore be subdivided as follows:

Ethos—ethical responsibility
Adult—objective data processing
Pathos—personal attractiveness and responsiveness

Berne has also described how the structural analysis can be extended in other directions. In the initial statement of the theory by Berne, particular modes of functioning were associated with particular organs. The *archeopsyche* primarily functions with internal programming, that is, endogenous biological forces organize the psychological processes. This leads to autistic behavior such as dreaming, fantasies, fugue states, delusional behavior, and involuntary ac-

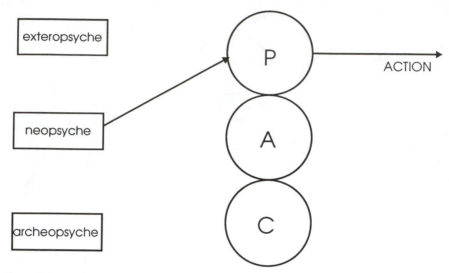

Figure 8.3   Programming ego states.

tions such as tics, mannerisms, and slips of the tongue. The *neopsyche* primarily functions with probability programming, that is, autonomous data processing organizes our psychological processes based upon our past experiences. This leads to reality-tested behavior such as activities (professions, trades, sports, and hobbies) and procedures (or data processing techniques). Finally, the *exteropsyche* primarily functions with external programming, that is from incorporated external rules (incorporated primarily from the parents). This leads to social behavior, such as rituals, ceremonies, pastimes, operations and maneuvers, games, and intimacy (terms that have specific meaning in Berne's theory of interpersonal interactions, called *transactional analysis*).

Although initially Berne associated each of these modes of functioning (which he calls determinants) to each kind of ego state, he felt that they could be independent. This means that the executive ego state could be the Child, Adult, or Parent, and the programming could be either internal, probability, or external, giving nine possibilities. For example, a person may be described as a probability-programmed Parent—perhaps a dictator who is authoritarian with rational (statistical) justification and who believes what he is saying (Figure 8.3).

When the Child ego state is functioning as a *Natural Child*, its programming is internal. When the Child ego state is functioning under the influence of the Parent ego state (the *Adapted Child*), the programming is external. The ethos of the Adult ego state is externally programmed whereas the pathos is internally programmed. Berne noted that the Parent ego state may be nurturing or prohibitive. If you do not accept Freud's notion of the death instinct, then the nurturing Parent ego state is internally programmed, whereas the prohibitive Parent ego state externally programmed. If you accept Freud's notion of the death instinct, then both Parent ego states are internally programmed, energized by libido and destrudo, respectively. Again, if one is looking for a psy-

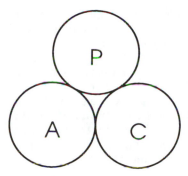

Figure 8.4 An alternative representation of the three ego states.

choanalytic analogy, internal programming is analogous to the psychoanalytic concept of primary process cognition (the type of cognition that traditionally presented Freudian theory sees as governing id-motivated cognition, such as dreams); probability programming is analogous to secondary process cognition (the type of cognition that governs ego-motivated cognition); and external programming is analogous to identification (desires introjected from parents).

The basic conceptual units that Berne defined gave him a reasonably large armamentarium with which to describe various psychological disorders. The following sections will look at four types of psychopathology using Berne's structural analysis.

Structural Pathology

Structural pathology is conceptualized in terms of deformities in the structure of the total personality. One ego state may govern exclusively. For example, if the Child ego state governs exclusively, excluding the Adult and Parent ego states completely, we may have a narcissistic impulsive personality (for example, that which a high-class prostitute might have) or an active schizophrenic. The Adult and Parent ego states are said, in this case, to be decommissioned. The Child ego state is experienced as the real self.

A second structural problem is *contamination*. One ego state intrudes through the other ego state's boundaries. For example, if the Adult ego state contaminates the Child ego state, delusions and hallucinations may occur. In the schizophrenic, the predominant ego state is that of the Child, and the hallucinations and delusions are intrusions from the Parent and Adult ego states, respectively. The Child ego state does not realize that it has been intruded upon because the boundaries are not firm enough to recognize the intrusion for what it is, i.e., that it comes from a source outside the Child ego state boundaries. (Actually Berne says that Child–Parent contamination is not possible, but he also says that hallucinations have their source in the Parent ego state. This is a contradiction. However, it would seem that Berne intentionally draws the Parent, Adult, and Child ego states on top of each other to emphasize that contamination is only possible, as he sees it, between Parent and Adult and between Child and Adult. Figure 8.4 shows an improved way of drawing the three ego states. Contamination of each ego state by any other is possible in the theory depicted in Figure 8.4).

Processes originating from the predominant ego state plus its contaminated areas are *ego-syntonic*, whereas processes originatcing from outside the boundary are *ego-dystonic*. (It is critical, therefore, to investigate whether hallucinations are ego-syntonic or ego-dystonic. Both types of hallucinations are probably possible.) In Berne's conceptualization, the Adult ego state can be contaminated both by the Child and by the Parent ego states.

Some additional illustrations may increase our understanding of how Berne applies his concepts to explaining pathology.

1. Mania results from structural pathology. In mild levels of mania (*hypomania*), the Child and the Adult ego states exclude the Parent ego state, and the Child dominates (or contaminates) the Adult but the Adult still has some influence. In mania proper, the Child excludes the Adult as well. However, the Parent ego state is still monitoring the person's behaviors, and the Child ego state knows it is being watched. Thus, the Child ego state may have delusions of reference and persecution (for example, that people are recording what is taking place). When the Child becomes exhausted, the Parent ego state assumes control and takes revenge, leading to severe depression.

2. Lesions in the boundary between two ego states lead to *boundary symptoms*, again a form of structural pathology. Lesions of the Child–Adult boundary lead to such symptoms as feelings of unreality, estrangement, depersonalization, jamais vu, and déjà vu.

3. Contamination is important in understanding the difference between dissociated thoughts and delusions. If a thought from the Child ego state becomes conscious to the Adult ego state, the Adult ego state experiences it as a strange idea, a dissociated thought. If however, a contamination has occurred and the Child thought comes from the contaminated area, then the thought is ego-syntonic and may be labeled (by others) as a delusion. The Adult ego state does not realize that it is a thought from outside of its boundary.

4. A person's ego states may be well defined with impermeable boundaries so that he is well organized. However, there may be severe internal conflicts in the ego states. For example, an alcoholic who can segregate his ego states well may be able to work effectively on his job despite heavy drinking at home.

This example raises an issue that Berne does not address clearly. Can there be several ego states that are Adult, or Child, or Parent? Berne describes contamination and other forms of structural pathology as occurring between two ego states from different organs. But, of course, each organ may have several ego states. For example, if the working alcoholic is one ego state and the drunk alcoholic is another, can these two states both be Adult or both be Child, or is one an Adult ego state and the other a Child? Berne is by no means clear on this issue.

5. Berne views the effects of electroconvulsive shock as leading to the Parent ego state being cathected, and the Adult suppresses the Child.
6. In character disorders, psychopathy, and paranoia the Adult ego state is contaminated by the Child ego state (and cooperates with it), but it is not decommissioned. This is similar to the state of affairs in hypomania and mild depression.
7. In neurosis, the Adult ego state is contaminated by the Child and Parent ego states, and the Parent ego state is the prime enemy. During free association, the Child ego state can talk while the Adult and Parent ego states listen. The censorship of the Parent ego state is suspended. (In contrast, during hypnosis and narcoanalysis the Adult and Parent ego states are temporarily decommissioned.)

Functional Pathology

Psychological disorder is described in terms involving the *lability* of cathexis (that is, the ease or difficulty in shifting from one ego state to another), and the *permeability* of ego state boundaries. For example, a person may show a stubborn resistance to shifting ego states, or may shift opportunistically. Ego state boundaries can be firm or soft, and the softer they are the easier contamination is. Cathexis may be *viscous*, which would make shifting ego states difficult. (What this term is supposed to mean other than that shifting is difficult is hard to imagine. It would have been easier to understand if Berne had simply said that some people are sluggish in shifting ego states, if that was all he meant.)

Content Pathology

Berne does not label a third source of pathology, but he implies one. He says that Parent, Adult, and Child ego states can all be syntonic with one another, with no contamination or functional pathology, yet there may be pathology. He gives the example of a happy concentration camp guard. We would see such a person as pathological, not because of any structural or functional pathology in his system of ego states, but because we object to the behaviors, desires, thoughts, and emotions he has. This example, suggests that the content of the ego states may be sufficient to cause pathology, especially if the psychologist or psychiatrist does not approve of the content of your ego states.

Conflict Pathology

A fourth source of psychopathology may occur if the executive ego state is programmed by a form of programming typical of other ego states. Berne, however, does not give specific types of psychopathology that results from this.

Discussion

What causes pathology? Berne says little about this except that trauma during childhood is responsible, a conventional psychoanalytic view. Because

A CASE OF A CHILD MOLESTER

Kasper, Baumann, & Alford, (1984) presented a structural analysis of a child molester that illustrates the use of Berne's concepts to understand people's behavior. Their client, Jerry, had been a noncommissioned officer in the military for 20 years. He had two sons, aged 19 and 16, and a 13-year-old daughter. He had been sentenced to 5 years for sodomy, indecent acts, and carnal knowledge involving his daughter.

Jerry was the first-born in a large family. His father worked on fishing boats and was absent for weeks at a time. During these absences, his mother, an alcoholic, would drink heavily and leave Jerry in charge of the family. She referred to Jerry as "her little man." Kasper suggested that Jerry learned from these experiences "Don't be close" and "Be strong—you have to take care of everyone," injunctions that became part of his script.

Eventually, social agencies stepped in and dispersed the children to various relatives. Jerry was sent to live with his paternal grandfather who was a minister. The grandfather taught Jerry strict fundamentalist beliefs, which included prohibitions against sexual activity. The grandfather was affectionate and spent time with Jerry, teaching him carpentry and fishing, but he also sexually abused Jerry. Kasper suggested that Jerry learned from the religious experiences "Be perfect," and from the sexual abuse, "Sex with children is ok."

Jerry was a very demanding husband and father, which led his wife to withdraw from him over the years. Jerry began to drink heavily as his wife withdrew, further alienating his wife. His daughter, however, remained close to Jerry, and he turned to his daughter for the love that he never received from his mother or from his wife, just as his grandfather had turned to him.

Jerry was an outgoing and friendly person, who performed well as a soldier and who was well thought of by his superiors. But he was lonely and had feelings of emptiness and lack of love. Kasper hypothesized that the "Don't be close" injunction leads people to withdraw from intimate relations with other adults for fear of rejection and is common in child molesters. Such people see relationships with children as the only "safe" relationships possible.

The sexual abuse that Jerry experienced as a child was associated with love, fun, excitement, and closeness. The behavior originated from his grandfather's Child ego state and was incorporated into the 8-year-old Jerry's ego states, now present in Jerry's Child ego state. Yet Jerry's Parent ego state had introjected the prohibitions against sexual activity of any kind, and so sex was acceptable only if it was childlike. Typically Jerry molested his daughter only when he was drunk, thus in his Child ego state with his Parent ego state decommissioned. Kasper summarized Jerry's structural analysis in Figure 8.5.

trauma is responsible, however, and because a child may experience several traumas, there is no reason why a person may not grow up with several Child ego states each with its organization and characteristics.

Berne's theory is obviously derived from psychoanalytic theory. His definition of ego states parallels the tripartite division of the psychic structure proposed by Freud. Yet his focus upon the complexity and organization of ego states makes them good examples of Angyalian subsystems. Furthermore, both Angyal and Berne talk of subsystem boundaries and of penetration and contamination of subsystems. Berne's concepts are able to generate a variety of possibilities for psychological disorders, thereby capturing the diversity of psychiatric illnesses quite well, in a way that the more abstract schema of Angyal does not. These descriptions develop the way in which Angyal's theory could be used to describe psychiatric disorders. Furthermore, as I noted in my comments on Jung's theory, Berne's general description of ego states provides illustrations of Angyal's abstract terms, such as *subsystem* and *subsubsystem*.

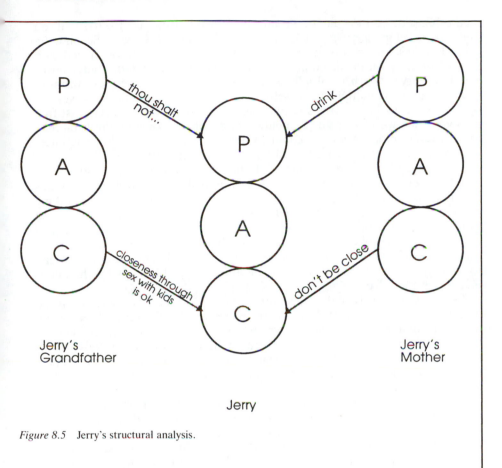

Figure 8.5 Jerry's structural analysis.

Berne's focus upon organized ego states seems to be a fruitful development from psychoanalytic theory, but the tendency for Berne's terminology to be distorted, or anthropomorphized, remains a problem. The proclivity of people to talk as if there really were ids and superegos inside people's minds is minimal compared to the tendency toward personification of Child, Adult, and Parent ego states. However, anthropomorphism in a theory may not be bad when the theory is used as a basis for psychotherapy, especially with clients who are not well-versed in psychological theory and who may be put off by jargon used in more formal theories of personality.

A VARIETY OF OTHER VIEWS

James Ogilvy: A Multiplicity of Selves

Ogilvy (1977), a philosopher, has criticized two ideal organizations of the mind. First, he argued against the notion that a single unified *self* exists, an idea espoused, he thought, by Freud (1933; a relatively fixed self), Erikson (1968; a developing self) and Lifton (1970; sequential selves). Second, he argued against theories in which a multiplicity of selves are organized as a social hierarchy with a single powerful self that rules the mind. Ogilvy advocated a theory in which a multiplicity of selves has a decentralized organization.

For Ogilvy, a multiplicity of selves, a pluralized pantheon of selves, as opposed to a single monotheistic ego leads to freedom. (He saw the least free person as one who has a single, highly predictable personality. Predictability, in his view, signifies lack of freedom.) Each self is a source of differing interpretations of the world, based on differing interpretive schemes.

These intrapersonal selves have different *personalities*. The person is the result of mediation among this collection of individual, relatively autonomous intrapersonal selves. The goal is to prevent any one of these selves from taking control as a monarch or single administrator. Ogilvy saw the ideal as the avoidance of a hierarchical organization of the selves. Instead, a *heterarchical organization* (McCulloch, 1965), illustrated by the coordination and integration of the different parts of the body, should prevail. Heterarchy does not lead to anarchy. The body, incidentally, is not simply a good analogy for the mind, it is one of the selves.

Ogilvy asked whether the subselves have still further selves and so on, ad infinitum, but decided that they did not. However, the different selves may all have individual ego-ideals, needs, personality traits, and so forth. For Ogilvy, the intrapersonal selves are projected onto mythic figures such as gods, and in turn, the intrapersonal selves are formed from introjected elements from past projections. Thus, we can expect certain commonalities in the intrapersonal selves of different people.

A weaker version of this model describes a person's behavior as the result of a succession of separate identities (or roles, or masks) that are assumed. Ogilvy preferred viewing the selves as working together, much as a group does to achieve a final product (behavior). Individual differences result from the different evolution of the multiple selves and their differing organization.

Sampson (1983), too, has argued for the usefulness of a multicentered self, as opposed to the integrated self proposed by some developmental psychologists, such as Erik Erikson (1968) and Jane Loevinger (1977).

Georges Gurdjieff: A Mystic

Ouspensky (1949) has described the teachings of Gurdjieff, an Armenian mystic, whom he met in the early part of this century in Russia. Many of Gurdjieff's ideas concerning the structure of personality are similar in many ways to the ideas presented here.

Early on Gurdjieff talked of a person containing many different people. He explains, for example, that people cannot keep promises because the "self" that makes the promise is not the same as the "self" that breaks the promise. Gurdjieff suggested that people change selves continually, seldom remaining the same for even 30 minutes. Each of these selves call themselves "I." They each consider themselves masters and do not like to recognize one another. Gurdjieff thought that there was no order among them. Whoever gets the upper hand is master until another seizes power.

These selves have separate minds, entirely independent of one another with separate functions and spheres in which they manifest themselves. These selves are mutually exclusive and incompatible. Thus, the whole never expresses itself, although each individual I calls itself by the name of the whole and acts in the name of the whole. One solution is for the many I's to elect a leader who can keep the other I's in their place and make each function at the appropriate time. The ultimate solution for Gurdjieff was for the person to develop a true master, a higher self who can control all of the lesser selves.

The I's are created by experiences and can be affected by external circumstances. Different situations call forth different I's. Thus, Gurdjieff's psychological perspective encompasses learning theory and situationism.

These many I's create many contradictions and are in constant conflict. If we were to feel all of these contradictions in one instant, we would feel what we really are, but we would also feel mad. If we cannot destroy the contradictions, we create buffers so that we cease to feel the contradictions. Buffers lessen shocks, but buffers also prevent us from waking up to the path to higher levels of consciousness where there is but a single and permanent I. Gurdjieff also drew a distinction between the self we present to others and the real self we are.

Later in his description of the path to higher levels of consciousness, Ouspensky describes the task of learning to observe oneself. While behaving, you must try to observe and remember yourself behaving. Self-observation is observation of the mask (c.f., Jung's concept of the persona), the part we unconsciously play and that we cannot stop playing. This division of attention (toward the outside world and toward yourself attending to the outside world) suggests another division of the the mind into selves. The self that we really are is *essence*, whereas the self that we have become because of external influences is our *personality*. (In Chapter 7, these subselves were called the real self and the facade self.) Infants have only essence, but education immediately creates the personality. Since our essence is often suppressed, it often proves to be on the level of a small child. Once the individual decides to move toward higher levels of functioning, the essence must be developed. A person's real I can be developed only from his essence.

Gurdjieff also phrased his ideas in terms of roles. Each person has a definite repertoire of roles that he or she plays in most circumstances. The repertoire of roles is limited to no more than five or six: one or two for family, one or two for work, one for social friends, and one for intellectual friends. When we are in a role, we are fully identified with the role. Without a role we feel undressed. (The proposition that we have five or six roles matches the number of selves proposed by other theorists, as discussed later in this chapter.)

Note that there is an inconsistency in Gurdjieff's thinking between the multitude of I's that change from moment to moment and the limited number of roles. This inconsistency can perhaps be resolved by reducing the number of I's and viewing them as having more than a momentary existence.

Decision Theorists: Self-Deception

Those concerned with rational decision-making, such as economists, psychologists, and philosophers, have been concerned with the ability of people to deceive themselves. Although Elster (1985) drew attention to inconsistencies in people's beliefs and wishes, he preferred the explanatory concept of mental compartmentalization rather than split selves. For others (for example, Pears, 1985), self-deception appears to involve two selves, the subject and the object of deception. Writers on this issue typically consider the problem to be one self ignoring the "truth" perceived by the other self. Pears warned against confusing these two selves with the conscious and the unconscious and suggested the concept of *functional isolation* instead. The subject-self contains elements that do not interact with all of the object-self's elements. The two systems can be conceptualized as overlapping circles. The desire to avoid accepting what the requirement of total evidence counsels causes this functional isolation (Davidson, 1985).

Others, in discussing the phenomenon of self-deception, have proposed a model of the mind of "the older medieval city, with relatively autonomous neighborhoods, linked by small lanes that change their names half way across their paths, a city that is a very loose confederation of neighborhoods of quite different kinds, each with its distinctive internal organization" (Rorty, 1985, p. 116). Rorty views the self as a loose configuration of habits, habits of thoughts, perception, motivation, and action, acquired at different stages, in the service of different ends. Margolis (1982) proposed that the person can be viewed as two selves, one concerned with selfish benefits and the other with group benefits.

Sidgwick (1893) drew attention to the temporal multiplicity of selves, namely that the I of the present moment may be very different from the I of the past or of the future, and we might note, in addition, that the individual occasionally regresses to the earlier versions of the self. Steedman and Krause (1985) talked of a multifaceted individual having different points of view, whereas others (de Sousa, 1976; Dennett, 1978; Hofstadter & Dennett, 1981; Lycan, 1981) have argued in favor of picturing the self as a hierarchical structure of ever-simpler homunculi. Finally, Elster (1985) proposed what may be a fitting analogy—the mind as a computer with different programs (software) being loaded and taking control at different times (such as SPSS[x] or Microsoft Word). To extend this analogy, we might suggest for subsubselves, say, the crosstabs routine of SPSS[x].

W. R. D. Fairbairn: Object-Relations Theory

Fairbairn (1954) is one of the group of psychoanalysts who have become known as object-relations theorists. Fairbairn proposed that the infant, when faced with a frustrating parent tries to control this aspect of his environment. In his mind, the infant splits the object into its good and bad aspects and introjects or internalizes the bad aspect. This makes the environment good and the infant bad. Even in extreme cases, abused children tend to see themselves as bad and their parents as good.

Fairbairn proposed also that these internalized aspects, or *objects*, become dynamic structures that are capable of acting as independent agents within the mind. These structures are located in the ego, and the situation is as if there were a multiplicity of egos at war with one another. Fairbairn called this the *endopsychic situation*.

Fairbairn also looked at these structures more abstractly. He described the *libidinal ego*, which is that part of the mind that feels needy, attacked, and persecuted; the *internal saboteur* (or antilibidinal ego, or attacking ego), which is aggressive and attacking especially toward the libidinal ego and resembles the classic Freudian superego; and the *central ego*, which tries to repress these subsidiary egos. (The internal saboteur also tries to repress the libidinal ego.)

The goal of psychotherapy is to make the bad objects conscious so that their emotional power can be dissolved. Fairbairn used dream analysis to assist this process. Fairbairn's technique of dream interpretation is similar to that of Perls (1969) in that each element of the dream is assumed to represented an ego structure.

Mardi Horowitz: States of Mind

Horowitz (1988) proposed the concept of a *state of mind*. A state of mind is a relatively coherent pattern, a composite of diverse forms of experience and expression that appear almost simultaneously. These states of mind are accompanied by characteristic expressive behaviors (such as the pace or tone of the voice and facial expressions).

Horowitz categorized these states of mind for the degree to which emotions and impulses were controlled: undermodulated, well-modulated, or overmodulated. Horowitz also suggested that one particular state of mind could sometimes try to co-exist with another, a notion that resembles Angyal's concept of the pressure one subsystem can exert on another in its effort to take control of the mind.

Horowitz suggested naming these states of mind so that they can be discussed with the client in psychotherapy and observed by the client when alone. This naming helps the client control the states, because the client can observe his or her mind moving from one state to another.

J. M. M. Mair: A Community of Selves

Mair (1977), a psychologist, has suggested that, rather than viewing the mind as an individual unit, we can consider the mind to a be a "community of selves." The expressions "to be of two minds" about an issue and "to do battle with ourselves" suggest that we sometimes talk and act as if we were two people rather than one. Gestalt therapy (Perls, Hefferline, & Goodman, 1951) includes exercises to enable us to explore these multiple selves.

Mair suggested that it is useful in psychotherapy to encourage people to conceptualize their mind as a community of selves, some of which may be persistent whereas others are transient, some isolates whereas others work as a team, some who appear on many occasions whereas others appear only rarely, and some of which are powerful whereas others are submissive.

Mair gave three clinical examples of individuals who were readily able to conceptualize their minds as a community of selves. One man used a political framework, viewing his mind as made up of a cabinet of ministers in a government. Another used the notion of political factions, whereas the third used the notion of a troupe of actors. The range of analogies used suggests that we may find useful concepts for understanding the mind from politics, group processes, diplomacy, debate, propaganda, industrial organizations, labor relations, international trade, law, theater, literature, arts, or science.

Mair stressed that he considered this to be a metaphor. Our minds sometimes behave *as if* they were communities of selves. He shrank from postulating that they are communities of selves.

Abraham Maslow: Syndromes

Abraham Maslow (1970), one of the important influences in the development of the field of humanistic psychology, whose ideas on the classification of needs we discussed in Chapter 3, urged a holistic approach to the study of personality. Behavior, he argued, is as an expression or creation of the whole personality, which in turn is the result of everything that has ever happened to it. Personality is composed of *syndromes*, that is, structured, organized, and integrated complexes of diverse specificities (behavior, thoughts, impulses, perceptions, and so on) that have a common unity. The total personality and the syndromes tend to be well-organized and to resist change, instead seeking to re-establish themselves after forced changes and to change as a whole because of tendencies to seek internal consistency. (*Syndrome* is a confusing term because in psychiatry it refers to a cluster of symptoms associated with a particular psychiatric disorder.)

Within each syndrome there are hierarchies of importance and clusterings. There are specificities whose occurrences are associated, that is, thoughts and impulses that are frequently found together. Maslow felt that to analyze these elements lower in the hierarchy of organization was similar to studying an object at different levels of magnification. For example, we may study the tendency to prejudice, which is a subsyndrome of the need for power, which is a subsyndrome of a general insecurity syndrome. Although such analyses examine atomistic elements, Maslow preferred to study the elements in context rather than in isolation.

Behavior is an expression of the whole integrated personality (and thus, an expression of all of the personality syndromes). Your laughter at a joke, for example, is affected by your intelligence, self-esteem, energy, and so on. It is an expression of your whole personality.

Marvin Minsky: Agencies of the Mind

Minsky (1986), cofounder of the artificial intelligence laboratory at MIT, proposes that there are *agencies of the mind*, by which he means any and all psychological processes. Although he grants that a view of the mind as made up of many selves may be valid, he suggests that this may be a myth that we construct.

However, when introducing the concept of agencies (a broad term that includes selves as one type of agency), Minsky (1986) does suggest several important questions to ask about agencies: How do agents work? What are they made of? How do they communicate? Where do the first agents come from? Are we all born with the same agents? How to make new agents and change old ones? What are the most important kinds of agents? What happens when agents disagree? How could networks of agents want or wish? How can groups of agents do what separate agents cannot do? What gives them unity or responsibility? How could they understand anything? How could they have feelings and emotions? How could they be conscious or self-aware? Not all of these questions, of course, apply to subselves. But the questions of origins, heredity, learning, character, authority, and competence are pertinent to subselves.

Stewart Shapiro: Subselves

Stewart Shapiro noted that we typically talk to ourselves (Shapiro & Elliott, 1976). Inner dialogues take place as conversations between various subselves, different parts of our self, with different distinct personal characteristics.

Shapiro attempts to listen for evidence of conflict in the patient during therapy and then tries to separate the different parts of the person involved in this conflict. Shapiro sees his role as that of coach or facilitator, that is, helping the subselves emerge and training the patient to deal with them in constructive ways. It is critical that none of the subselves be rejected. Each must be understood and integrated back into the self-organization.

Shapiro tries to identify or develop a mediator for the subselves. He may call it a chairman of the board, or some term best suited for the particular patient. The goal is to transfer energy and power to this mediator (c.f., the ego in psychoanalysis and the Adult ego state in transactional analysis).

Subself therapy differs from a therapy such as transactional analysis because it permits the patient to identify and label the subselves, rather than fitting them into a predetermined set of subselves (such as Child, Adult, and Parent ego states).

Shapiro felt that the optimal number of subselves was between four and nine. Too many subselves results in a fragmented or chaotic self and is a form of psychological pathology.

Five kinds of subselves are found in most people:

1. *A nurturing parent subself.* This self supports and gives love, care, attention, praise, and positive reinforcement.

2. *An evaluative parent subself*. This self is often called the Critic, Pusher, or Voice of Authority. It reflects the norms and values of the society and sets up standards and measures you to see if you have lived up to them.
3. *A central organizing subself*. An Executive, Chairman, or Coordinator, who is the self that often works with the Observer and should act as the leader, though it is often displaced by other subselves, such as the Critic.
4. *A good, socialized, adapted child subself*. This is an obedient, conforming child who tries to please authorities. If this subself is too strong, it can lead to overconformity, role obedience, and lack of creativity.
5. *A natural child subself*. This subself is creative, nonconforming, rebellious, spontaneous, and playful.

Subselves can be introjected subselves. For example, there may be an Audience (or Other people), and there can be internalized parents, such as a Mother.

These subselves can interact in a *drama* (or life script), as a *family*, as an *organization* or *task group*, or as a *discussion group*. It is important for the psychological health of the client for the subselves to get along with one another. An internal civil war or great conflict and tension can lead to psychological disturbance. The group of subselves should be democratic, with a minimal amount of partisanship, favoritism, and moralistic judgments. The energy of the subselves should also be rechanneled away from fighting into constructive problem-solving under the leadership of the Chairman. In addition, the Observer should be developed to act as a consultant to the total self-group.

The Performer versus the Pusher is a common conflict. The Performing Child or Performer is the subself who puts on a performance of some kind, and the Pusher, or Slave driver, demands that the Performer perform. This often makes the Performer rebel against performing, resulting in conflict. (The Performer may in fact have two subselves, the socialized child and the natural child.) The Pusher is often associated with a Critic too.

In marital conflicts, we often externalize this inner conflict. We project one of our subselves onto the partner and fight with it in the marriage relationship instead of internally.

Shapiro identified several different types of psychopathology:

1. Too many subselves, leading to inner chaos.
2. Too great an inner conflict, especially where the Chairman has little power.
3. Negative emotions (such as sadness and depression) are often caused by one subself attacking the Child, often without the patient's awareness.
4. Although Shapiro does not mention this, it could well be that one subself has pathological content.

Psychological health involves having an effective Chairman, who can observe, coordinate and execute decisions, and promote basic harmony among the subselves. However, Shapiro notes that integrating the subselves is not enough. We have various subselves, but we are not them. We are greater than the sum of the parts. We have to dis-identify with our subselves eventually, and transcend them. We have to achieve a higher level of awareness—a spiritual harmony that is beyond the psychological harmony.

John Rowan: Subpersonalities

Rowan's (1990) preference is for the term *subpersonality*, and he defines it as "a semi-permanent and semi-autonomous region of the personality capable of acting as a person" (p. 8). Rowan noted that it is necessary, on the one hand, to reify subpersonalities, but on the other hand, to remember that we are not talking about things but about processes that are fluid and in change.

In discussing the origin of subpersonalities, Rowan suggested that roles could bring out accompanying subpersonalities. Internal conflicts, in which two or more sides argue within us also can lead to the formation of subpersonalities. Our bodies can also participate in these conflicts and act antagonistically to our mind. Thus, the body, or parts of the body, can also be regarded as subpersonalities. Identification with heroes or heroines can sometimes lead to the person taking on the identity of the hero. Subpersonalities can also derive from the Freudian personal unconscious and the Jungian collective unconscious.

In a simple study of subpersonalities, Rowan asked the members of a group he led to describe their subpersonalities. At the first meeting, the number described ranged from 0 to 18 with a mean of 6.5. In later discussions, occasional participants did not seem to have any limit on the number of possible subpersonalities. Other participants could describe subpersonalities from earlier stages of development but felt that those were fading and no longer important. Rowan felt that 4 to 8 was the normal range. Some participants felt comfortable giving names or labels to their subpersonalities, whereas others did not.

The next question addressed by Rowan was whether some subpersonalities might be held in common by many people. Answering this question is by no means easy. Classic theories of personality and psychotherapy provide abstract labels for subpersonalities held in common, such as Perls's (1969) top dog/bottom dog or Berne's (1961) Parent, Adult, and Child ego states. But there may also be more concrete subpersonalities held in common. An analogy here is provided by Steiner's (1974) discussion of scripts in transactional analysis. As well as the abstract scripts of no mind (crazy), no love (depression), and no pleasure (drug abuse), Steiner also described specific scripts such as *playboy*, *jock*, and the *woman behind the man*. Allison and Schwartz (1980) classified subpersonalities into persecutors, rescuers, and internal self-helpers. Rowan himself did not propose a classification of subpersonalities.

Working with a client in psychotherapy can profitably use subpersonalities. Clients, if they like this conceptualization, must first identify and accept their subpersonalities. Rowan, following Assagoli (1975), suggests that the next phases are coordination, integration, and synthesis. However, since each subpersonality is an expression of ourselves and need not be harmful (unless they control us), synthesis may not be necessary.

Rowan did propose a developmental sequence for subpersonalities. The infant begins as one unified whole. As Rogers (1981) suggested, the child then differentiates between the part approved of by the parents and the part they disapprove of. The OK regions and the not-OK regions then split into sub-regions as the child matures, and then the childhood regions, especially the not-OK regions, may become closed off (repressed) under the societal (and parental) pressure. Following Jung (Progoff, 1973), Rowan believes that one or more *persona* and a *shadow* develop, as well as a *patripsych*, a concept borrowed from Southgate and Randall (1978), who define it as an internal constellation of patriarchal patterns—attitudes, ideas, and feelings that develop in relation to authority and control and that are internalized from the culture in which we live. Because the real self is closed off, the person typically feels hollow. There is no center, and the person must rely on the persona developed to deal with others. At this point psychotherapy is beneficial.

Rowan urges research into such issues as the number, type, and common qualities of the subpersonalities held by people and their structure (egalitarian or hierarchical, communes or committees, etc.). He also puts forward several propositions based on the principles of group dynamics, in which the term *group member* is replaced by *subpersonality*.

1. Better decisions are made by bringing out and exploring the subpersonalities and by integrating, rather than allowing one subpersonality to dominate, and by making compromises.
2. It is useful to develop one subpersonality to be a trained observer and to give feedback to the group of subpersonalities on the style in which they relate to one another.
3. Disturbances in the interactions and conflict should be given priority for exploration and should not be ignored.
4. Different situations call for different types of leaders, and so each subpersonality may have usefulness for some problems. The goal is to use the subpersonalities rather than be used by them.
5. The subpersonalities will change as they interact more and trust one another more.
6. No one subpersonality can represent or speak for the whole group.

PERSONAL USE OF THE CONCEPT

The concept of subselves is one which people find easy to use. For example, in the set of films in which a client Gloria is interviewed by Carl Rogers, Frederick Perls, and Albert Ellis the metaphor of subselves is present in all interviews (Shostrum, 1965).

With Carl Rogers, Gloria talks of her "shady side" and her "ornery devilish side." She also talks of splits in her self. "I want to approve of me always, but my actions won't let me," to which Rogers comments that "It sounds as if your actions are kind of outside of you. . . . It sounds like a triangle, doesn't it? You feel that I or other therapists in general or other people say 'It's all right,

THE DISUNITY OF THE SELF

Angyal proposed that the total system called the mind could be viewed as made up of several subsystems. In more common terms, we could call these subsystems *subselves*. Lester (1992) asked whether people were able to use this notion in order to describe themselves. He studied 44 students enrolled in a course on abnormal psychology. (He wanted students that had some familiarity with psychology, yet that were not familiar with Angyal's ideas.) He asked the students the following question:

Almost all people feel that there are different sides to their personality. We have different roles or different selves depending on the situation or on our mood. I want you to take some time to think about your different selves. How many can you identify and what are their characteristics? Give each a name/title and describe it in three or four adjectives.

Thirty-seven students completed the task.

The students identified an average of 3.5 selves (with a standard deviation of 1.3). The range was 2 to 6. The men reported fewer selves than the women (2.5 versus 3.8), but the number identified was not related to age. Students with higher extraversion scores and higher neuroticism scores tended to identify more selves—neurotic extraverts identified 4.6 selves, compared to 3.2 for students in other groups.

The students took different approaches to describing these selves. Some used role titles, such as professional self, wife/mother, and student. Some used labels such as cerebral, social, passive, anxious, and loving, whereas others used phrases, such as "Around people I know I am more talkative, friendly, funny; when I don't know anyone I'm always afraid of making a fool out of myself so I'm quiet."

natural enough. Go ahead.' I guess you feel your body sort of lines up on that side of the picture, but something in you says, 'But I don't like it that way unless it's really right.'"

We seem to have a part of Gloria that passes judgment on another part. She has a body and actions that do one thing, and a part of her mind that argues for an alternative course of action.

With Perls, Gloria exhibits the two polarities of her existence—the mother, treating others as if they were her children, afraid to be close, and at the other extreme, the little girl, hiding in a corner, waiting to be rescued, but willing to be close.

With Ellis, Gloria again refers to parts of herself. She fears showing "stinky part of me" to others, and Ellis tells that she is taking a part of herself and acting as if was the total self. He tells her that she must accept herself with the defective part.

Finally, in the summary interview with Everett Shostrom, Gloria says that she felt her more lovable, caring self with Rogers, but that he would make it hard for her spitfire self to come out. Shostrom comments that she "felt your feeling self with Dr. Rogers, your fighting self with Dr. Perls" and she finishes for him "and my thinking self with Dr. Ellis."

Rather than selves, Gloria sometimes refers to "sides," but Shostrom moves to using the notion of subselves to describe Gloria's experiences with the three therapists.

THEORETICAL PROPOSITIONS ABOUT SUBSELVES

Subselves as a Small Group

Lester (1985, 1993/1994) suggested the usefulness of viewing the various subselves in the mind as a small group. In group dynamics research, intragroup conflict is typically seen as counterproductive, expending energy on activities that are unrelated to the group purpose. For example, in Cattell's (1948) group syntality theory, the energy expended on establishing and maintaining cohesion and harmony in the group is called *maintenance synergy*, while that used to achieve the goals of the group is called *effective synergy*. The more energy goes into maintenance, the less is available for achieving goals.

Interestingly, as we saw earlier in this chapter, Shapiro and Elliott (1976) demonstrated the usefulness in psychotherapy of creating new subselves in clients designed to reduce this intragroup conflict. For example, it is useful to have a subself that has the function of recording secretary for information storage, another with the function of mediator and sometimes a chairman of the board with executive power to help resolve conflict between the subselves. We might add that occasional subselves may outlive their usefulness and should be encouraged to retire, i.e., no longer try to influence the individual's mind.

Lester noted that small groups with a hierarchical structure are often more productive, but their members are less satisfied. On the other hand, some structure is often useful. The goal is perhaps to have a dominant subself, but not one that is overly dominating. In transactional analysis (Berne, 1961), each ego state has periods that it is in control of the mind (at which time the other ego states are said to be *decommissioned*), but each ego state has an opportunity to control the mind at times (in Eric Berne's 1961 terminology, to be *cathected*).

Lester also noted that research on group dynamics indicates that increasing the size of the group eventually increases the chances that a dominant member will emerge and force conformity from the other groups members. Thus, there is a limit to the size of a group for effective functioning. In writing on subselves, Allport (1961), Rowan (1990), and Shapiro & Elliott (1976) have suggested that from 4 to 10 subselves is ideal.

Lester noted that research on group dynamics indicates that egalitarian small groups typically produce more and better solutions to problems than individuals, but that they take longer to reach decisions and are more likely to make decisions that are risky. Perhaps these same principles might apply to people with many subselves. For example, it was proposed by both Andras Angyal (1965), Eric Berne (1961), and Carl Jung (Progoff, 1973) that subselves that are excluded from ever assuming control of the mind exert pressure on the dominant (and domineering) subself, often intruding upon (and even invading) the dominant subself, leading to psychological disturbance.

Balance

Boulding (1968), in writing about the subsystems of society, noted that each system tends to the create the need for an opposing system that balances it and that typically these two subsystems share similar characteristics. A forceful pro-choice movement for abortion leads to the development of a forceful pro-life anti-abortion movement, and vice versa. Racketeering employers and racketeering unions go together.

Lester (1987b), following Jung, noted that this might occur in subselves. As we saw earlier in this chapter, Jung (Progoff, 1973) felt that each complex in conscious mind was balanced by a complementary complex in the unconscious mind with opposed traits. For example, if the conscious complex is extroverted and prone to use intuition, then the unconscious complex will be introverted and prone to use sensing. Freeing this idea from the polarity of conscious/unconscious, we can propose that any subself will tend to encourage the development of another subself with complementary characteristics. An example is the description of the "top dog" and "bottom dog" by Perls, Hefferline, and Goodman (1951) in their description of gestalt therapy.

Integration

If the mind is conceptualized as being made up of several subselves, the issue arises as to how the mind might be integrated (see Chapter 6). It might be that the process of integration (seen by both Erik Erikson, 1959, and Carl Jung, as described in Progoff, 1973, as the task of the second half of life) involves breaking down the boundaries between the subselves and integrating them into a single unified self. Alternatively, it might be that the different subselves are fully developed and co-exist in harmony with one another as Berne (1961) and Shapiro and Elliott (1976) have described.

Types of Subselves

There have been many proposals for the types of subselves that might exist. Some theorists have suggested that there is a core self (Kelly, 1955) and a social self (Laing, 1969), a pseudo-self (Rogers, 1959), and a false self or a facade self (Wagner, 1971). It seems wrong to single out one of the subselves as a core self and also to have only one facade self. It seems more reasonable to propose several subselves that are equivalent (though differing in their influence on behavior), in much the same way as a person can have several roles without one being seen as a core role and the others as facade roles.

DISCUSSION

The notion that the mind may be usefully conceptualized as comprising several subselves is increasingly found among theorists. Although the notion was proposed by earlier theorists, it rarely assumed a major part in their theories, with the exception of Angyal's (1965).

Several principles have been proposed here for this set of subselves. The *principle of size* has suggested that people function best with from 4 to 10 subselves. The *principle of balance* has suggested that subselves tend to lead to the formation of complementary subselves with opposite traits. The *principle of integration* has suggested that healthy development may lead to the integration of the various subselves into one unified whole or to mutual co-existence between the subselves.

Much work remains to be done on classifying the types of subselves, because each theorist has proposed different classifications and different contents for the subselves. In psychotherapy, however, it appears more useful to permit clients to choose their own terms and analogies for describing their subselves. Research and principles from group dynamics research may also be a source of ideas for building a theory of the mind based on subselves.

9

Other Holistic Theories

There are many other theories of personality that are holistic in nature. Some have been proposed by those interested in theories of personality per se, whereas others have been proposed by those interested in systems of psychotherapy or some other field of psychology, such as social psychology. This chapter reviews the ideas of some of these minor holistic theories.

What makes these particular theories minor? Some are minor because, although they were were once considered important theories, they failed to attract enough psychologists interested in developing them or in conducting research on them, with the result that the psychological community lost interest in the theories except as critical steps in the development of modern psychology. Some are minor because the theories are not detailed enough to present a comprehensive theory of the structure of the mind. Others are minor because the authors were primarily interested in the therapeutic treatment of disturbed individuals, and so they are primarily known for their writings on therapy.

Nonetheless, their theories indicate that the holistic perspective of the mind is a major perspective. Furthermore, the particular theories reviewed briefly here introduce alternative terms and definitions of terms already introduced in this book earlier that may appeal to some of you. Authors of theories and researchers may, in the future, choose to base their ideas on these particular theories rather than those reviewed earlier in this book. Thus, it is important to be aware of these theories.

GORDON ALLPORT

Gordon Allport noted that the most important fact about personality was that it had a relatively enduring and unique *organization*, and the critical question concerned its structure and composition. This proposition clearly cast Allport as a holistic theorist. Indeed, he specifically rejected the approach that a personality was merely a sum of certain elements.

Allport (1937) reviewed many possible definitions of personality, and settled for this one:

Personality is the dynamic organization within the individual of those psycho-physical systems that determine his unique adjustment to his environment. (p. 48.)

Personality is organized, but it is constantly evolving and changing, and hence, dynamic. Allport (1955) called this process *becoming* and *individuation*. (Jung also used the term *individuation* in this sense—see Chapter 8.) Allport saw the essential nature of people as pressing toward a relative unification of life, which may never be fully achieved. The term *psycho-physical* was used to note that personality is neither exclusively neural nor mental. Body and mind are fused into a personal unity.

All behaviors proceed from this central and unified personality, and so the behaviors, which must be harmonious among themselves, give clues as to the organization of the personality. However, psychologists must take care to focus more on the organization of the personality than on the peripheral observable behaviors. Allport also noted that a particular behavior may be determined by very different personality organizations. Behaviors may be *phenotypically* similar (that is, look alike), but *genotypically* different (that is, have different causes).

Allport outlined his position more precisely by stating what he rejected in other ideas. For example, he was firmly opposed to typologies, citing them as too limited and lacking in ability to deal with each person's uniqueness. He also rejected explanations based solely on conditioned reflexes and instincts. *Drives*, which he defined as vital impulses leading to reduction of localized organic tensions, were inadequate to explain adult motivation, but were seen as more important for the motivation of young infants. (Allport felt that the infant lacks personality, which cannot develop until the human organism meets the environment, acts upon it, and is acted upon by it.)

The Child

Personality is not formed at birth, but it begins at birth. Personality is unstructured at birth, which in some sense implies unity, but it is also unorganized. Young infants seem not to be aware of their selves. They have no bodily, social or material self. The boundary between me and not-me is not yet established. Until infants can conceptualize themselves as independent people, they cannot develop their own personalities.

In the child, differentiation occurs. Specialized skills and adaptive responses develop. Patterns of behavior become more differentiated and more efficient. But differentiation is slow. When children are pleased, they jump up and down. The whole body is involved. Eventually precise adaptive movements replace these gross activities, as inhibition becomes possible. Allport did not like the description of stages of development. He felt that there is one uninterrupted course of development.

Structure of Personality

Allport distinguished five levels in the structure of personality:

1. Conditioned reflexes: simple learned forms of adaptive behavior
2. Habits: integrated systems of conditioned responses
3. Traits: dynamic and flexible dispositions resulting in part from the integration of specific habits

4. Selves: systems of traits with coherence
5. Personality: the progressive final integration of all the systems of response

Allport (1955) added another level to his hierarchy, called *intentions*, complex core characteristics of personality. Intentions are rather like a philosophy of life or a value system (perhaps analogous to what Andras Angyal called a system principle—see Chapter 6). These have a dynamic effect on our changing personality and set the goals toward which we strive. The unfinished structure of our personality has a dynamic power, tending toward closure as we age.

Most of us can be characterized by a few major intentional characteristics, unique for each of us, which guide the smaller units of our personality so that they are consistent with these major intentions.

The Proprium

Allport used the term *proprium* for the core self. "The proprium includes all aspects of personality that make for inward unity" (Allport, 1955, p. 40); it is "the central interlocking operations of the personality" (Allport, 1955, p. 54). It appears to exclude inherited dispositions and characteristics acquired by learning such as reflexes, habits, skills, and cultural values (unless these become integrated into the proprium).

Allport gave the proprium eight properties: (a) a bodily sense, i.e., streams of sensation from within the organism, (b) a self-identity, (c) ego-enhancement, a self-seeking tendency, (d) ego-extension through possessions, loved objects, ideal causes, and loyalties, (e) a rational agent, (f) a self-image, both what we are and what we aspire to, (g) propriate strivings that maintain rather than reduce tension, similar to Maslow's growth motives, and that make for the unification of the personality, and (h) a knower, a cognizant self that transcends these other functions.

Traits

Allport is most well-known for his focusing on traits, but many textbooks misrepresent his position on this concept. Allport is often called a trait theorist because he also became interested in measuring traits that are found to be *common* to all people. However, this was a side issue. Allport defined a trait as a "generalized and focalized neuropsychic system (peculiar to the individual)" with the capacity to "initiate and guide consistent . . . forms of adaptive and expressive behavior" (Allport, 1937, p. 295).

Traits for Allport are unique for each person, and a trait is an *organized subsystem in the personality*. It is similar to the subsystem of Angyal and the complex of Jung. In his later writings, he changed the term to *personal disposition*.

All traits are directive tendencies, but not all directive tendencies are traits. Traits are generalized and enduring; they have less to do with fleeting mental sets than with lasting processes such as interests, tastes, complexes, sentiments, and ideals. Traits result from an integration of numerous specific habits and a fusion of these habits with endowment. A trait forces the formation of new habits, useful for the trait, thereby transcending its specific foci of origin. Traits become autonomous motivational systems basic to the personality. No two people ever have precisely the same trait.

Attitudes are different—they have a well-defined object of reference. The more numerous the objects that arouse an attitude, the more similar an attitude is to a trait. The more specific and stimulus-bound an attitude is, the less it resembles a trait. Traits are general. Attitudes imply acceptance or rejection of the object. Traits have no such clear-cut direction. Between them, however, traits and attitudes cover virtually every type of disposition in the mind.

Traits are always changing and depend closely on the fluid conditions of the environment. Indeed, to be successful, traits must be dynamic and capable of changing. Traits can also be *directive* (or motivational) or *stylistic* (or expressive). (Expressive traits generally have a greater unconscious component.) Traits can also overlap, that is, they are interdependent, and they can also be in conflict. A trait is identified, not by a clean-cut boundary, but rather by a nuclear focus.

A trait can become so pervasive and dominant in someone's life that it is called a *cardinal* trait. More often, several *central* traits direct the personality, supported by a number of *secondary* traits. Allport felt that people have a limited number of traits, perhaps 5 to 10. (This is reminiscent of the discussion in Chapter 8 of the ideal number of subselves for a healthy mind.)

The Environment

Allport, of course, did not neglect the influence of the environment. Allport noted that an environment that places few demands on a person makes it easier to develop an integrated unified personality. The stresses of life may make it difficult (if not impossible) to adequately integrate a personality. Sometimes there is inertia in the person that impedes integration. Integration requires a strong desire in the person or an insistent demand from the environment for change.

Under strong environmental pressures, regression, in which the personality reverts to an earlier level of integration, may sometimes occur. Dissociation may take place when a self-coherent system in the personality fails to integrate with the remaining parts of the personality. Sometimes *infantilism*, or a failure to develop, occurs.

Functional Autonomy

Allport noted that people's motives are almost infinitely varied, in form and substance, and are self-sustaining. New motives grow out of antecedent systems but become functionally independent of them—the *principle of functional autonomy*. A developed person has a variety of autonomous motives. Functionally autonomous motives tend to be highly propriate, that is, well anchored to the self, to the extent of sometimes constituting the self.

Allport saw self-aggrandizement as a strong human motive, the desire to be appreciated and to have esteem. From this comes the development of a social self (a persona) that protects us from unwelcome narcissistic wounds. Allport also noted that we often deceive our conscious self. Thus, we find Allport accepting the familiar divisions of the mind into the conscious and unconscious selves, the real and facade selves, the body and mental selves, and an introjected self (the *socius*).

However, Allport did not dwell on these dichotomies to the same extent as did other theorists. For example, he viewed the unconscious as an abstraction referring to all the operations that fashion personality without the person's direct knowledge, but he felt that psychoanalysis places far too much emphasis upon its role. Allport viewed the unconscious-conscious dichotomy more like a figure–ground distinction—the conscious is what is in focus while the unconscious is what is in the background. No matter how unified and self-contained a personality is, it is always open at every moment to the surrounding environment. It acts upon and is acted upon by the environment. Tension, which always exists, heightens consciousness.

Unity

Allport saw the mind as a unified system, and he considered which factors help provide this unity. The baby has a primitive unity because it has not yet differentiated. However, once differentiation takes place, then *integration* must occur between the various parts. *Homeostasis*, especially physiological homeostasis, in which the system tends to persist in a steady state and to preserve it, leads to a static kind of unity. In *convergence*, one task comes to dominate the person and this provides a temporary unity, much as a *cardinal trait* facilitates a more long-term unity. Allport also noted that the very term *self*, a sense of which evolves in each of us as we develop, implies unity. The mature person can be self-objective and has a unifying philosophy of life (c.f., Angyal's version of the general system principle discussed in Chapter 6).

Discussion

As mentioned above, many presentations of Allport's ideas minimize the holistic aspects of his theory, focusing instead on his development of the concept of trait. From there, the writer typically moves on to the measurement of traits by modern psychological tests and the formal concepts of reliability and validity in modern measurement theory (e.g., McAdams, 1994). Although measurement issues interested Allport to some extent, we must not ignore the fact that Allport's concept of a trait was very similar to the notion of a subsystem or subself; for example, a cardinal trait can be seen as analogous to a core role for a person.

Furthermore, integration of the structures of the mind into a unified whole was seen by Allport as a major goal for humans, and his term for this unified whole, the *proprium*, is identical to what Jung called the *self*.

THE THEORY AND THE THEORIST

In comparing Freud's theory with Mowrer's theory in Chapter 3, it was noted that, in each case, the theory was appropriate for the era in which it was devised and for the theorist who devised it. Freud's theory was a reaction against the repressiveness of Europe during the Victorian era and was consistent with his life experiences, while Mowrer's theory was a reaction against the "anything goes" era of the 1960s and was consistent with his life experiences.

Atwood and Tomkins (1976) suggested that this was a general principle—that every theorist views human behavior from his or her perspective and so is influenced by his or her own life experiences. They presented several examples. Gordon Allport seems to have been strongly influenced in his life by his elder brother, Floyd, and by feelings of inferiority developed in childhood. His choices, therefore, were "functionally dependent" upon these childhood experiences, yet his theory argued for the "functional autonomy" of adult motives, as if trying to deny the impact of his childhood experiences. Indeed, in his autobiography he scarcely mentions his childhood.

Wilheim Reich's life and work were driven by a need to save humanity from the destructive effects of repressed sexuality. As a child, Reich idolized his mother, but discovered that she was having an affair with his tutor. He was so shocked that he told his father about it, after which his mother committed suicide. In betraying his mother, Reich was following his father's strict moral code, and his theory (and life's work) can be seen as act of atonement for his act of betrayal.

Carl Rogers (Chapter 7) stressed the role of conditional positive regard from the parents in forcing the child to suppress, and eventually repress, the real self, and to be what the parents appear to want their child to be. Atwood and Tomkins pointed out that this seems to have characterized Rogers's own childhood, and it was not until he went off to college that he was able to free himself from their conditions of worth.

Finally, Atwood and Tomkins described the connection between Carl Jung's focus on two attitudes toward experience, introversion versus extroverison (Chapter 8) and his own struggle between the two sides of his personality, which he labeled the number 1 personality and the number 2 personality. The number 1 personality was the child which everyone saw, the child who had difficulty in school and felt inferior to other children. The number 2 personality was the hidden inner self who was fascinated by the mysteries of the cosmos. Jung's adolescence and adulthood were dominated by the conflict between these two personalities. For example, the number 1 personality wanted financial security while the number 2 personality was interested in philosophy, and his choice of psychiatry was a compromise.

Atwood and Tomkins suggest that the dependence of theories of personality upon subjective factors, such as the theorists' life experiences, makes it difficult to devise a theory of personality sufficiently general to include and unify all of the different contributions. They also suggest that this problem does not plague the natural sciences. I think that they are overly pessimistic in this assessment. After all, the aim of the present book has been to show that the many theories of personality presented here can be subsumed under three major theories that, in themselves, are not incompatible. Furthermore, I think that they may be wrong in their assumption that theories in the natural sciences do not have this subjective elements. Many physicists, Einstein for one, disliked the introduction of probability concepts into the theories, saying that God did not play with dice. It may well be that such choices in natural science theories can also be related to the subjective epxeriences of the theorists.

KURT GOLDSTEIN

Kurt Goldstein (1963a, 1963b) proposed a theory of personality based upon his experience with the behavior and rehabilitation of brain-damaged patients. He felt that pathological phenomena are modifications of a normal process and, hence, can indicate the lawfulness of the normal process. (It is a common assumption in psychology that we can come to an understanding of psychological processes by exploring how they break down or how they manifest themselves in alternative organisms, such as lower animals.)

Goldstein's major assumption is that the person functions as a whole. Despite the fact that often our work with clinical patients or with animals in a laboratory situation suggests that discrete, circumscribed, disparate disturbances can be observed, Goldstein felt that this conclusion was wrong and a result of observing the organism in an abnormal situation. Symptoms resulting from pathology or laboratory manipulation are not isolated phenomena. Rather, they are solutions tried by the modified organism to cope with the new specific demands. The symptoms are expressions of the total organism and involve widespread changes. In a similar vein, Goldstein considered mind and body to be merely different aspects of unitary life process.

Furthermore, the behavior of this integrated organism can not be studied without taking into account the environment in which the organism dwells. (Goldstein preferred to talk of the organism, but we could substitute the words human, person, or individual in almost all instances.) The organism is continually coming to terms with environmental stimuli, producing *performances*, which are a product of the total organism. "Each effective performance (or each failure) is an integrated feature in a definite total behavior pattern" (Goldstein, 1963a, p. 36). In contrast, under physical and mental shock, brief, disordered, and inconsistent performance may appear—the so-called *catastrophic reactions*—in which organisms work toward shrinking their environment in order to reduce the demands made upon the organism. Under stress, the organism tries to achieve optimal performance, especially to preserve the functioning of the whole organism.

All performances show a figure–ground effect, in which one part of the performance stands out to the observer (the figure) whereas other parts are ignored (the ground). But the ground is present, even if it goes unnoticed. Goldstein's holistic position made him regard such phenomenon as drives, reflexes, or instincts as abstracted from very involved processes. Such phenomena are gross simplifications made from observations on organisms in grossly abnormal emergency situations.

Goldstein noted that the system is never at rest, but is in a continual state of excitement. Any stimulus produces changes in the organism as a whole, although we may observe changes in a more or less circumscribed area. However, because we observe a change in performance in this circumscribed are does *not* mean that changes do not occur elsewhere in the system, for the total system must remain "balanced."

In contrast, therefore, pathological conditions involve isolation of psychological processes and the prevention of integrated unitary performances. This leads to: (a) abnormally strong reactions in the isolated part of abnormal duration; (b) a closer binding of the reaction to the stimulus causing isolation (resulting in a stronger dependence of the pathological organism on external stimuli, or to compulsions if the stimulus is internal); (c) abnormal rigidity; or (d) alternating and oscillating reactions to a stimulus.

The mind is differentiated into part members, but it does not consist of these members. The members do not struggle against each other, nor does the whole struggle against the members. The members we distinguish neither compose the mind, nor are they antagonistic to it.

Goldstein felt that the energy supply to organisms is constant so that, if one performance requires great energy expenditure, then other performances suffer. For example, when thinking, we tend to be inattentive to sensory experiences. Since the whole organism is involved in any performance, only one performance is possible at a given moment. After a performance, if no new stimulation occurs, the organism returns to a state of equilibrium, an equalization process between the excitation in near and distant parts.

Goldstein categorized performances into those that are essential for the preservation of life (survival importance) and those that are essential to our nature (functional significance). In addition, the individual has to come to terms with the environment. Optimal performance requires a complete integration of the organism—*centering*—and adaptation to the environment. This occurs only on rare occasions. In particular, pathological processes are nonoptimal performances. Mild catastrophic reactions occur continually and inevitably as the organism comes to terms with the world, and so transient nonoptimal performance often occurs.

Catastrophic (or disordered) behavior is accompanied by *anxiety*. Anxiety is the experience of danger or of peril to one's self or one's existence. In fear, there is an object for us to deal with. With anxiety, there is no clear way to deal with the source, since the source is obscure. We try to flee without knowing where to flee. Anxiety occurs when we can no longer cope with a task in a way that preserves our essential nature. It is a result of disordered functioning, not merely a reaction to an object.

The normal person often has the urge to diminish anxiety by flight, or by the tendency toward order, norms, continuity, and homogeneity. But the normal person also has the urge for new experiences, the conquest of the world, and an expansion of its sphere of activity. Behavior oscillates between these two tendencies. The tendency toward actualization is primal, but involves conflict with the environment and, hence, shock and anxiety.

Each organism has its own characteristic environment or milieu. This *adequate milieu* is appropriate to our nature. Environments that cause catastrophic reactions are not adequate milieus. Disturbed individuals encounter non-adequate milieus more often than normal people since their normal reactions are impaired.

Tendency to Self-Actualization

Goldstein proposed that organismic life was governed by only one principle, which always remains the same (what Angyal called the *system principle*—see Chapter 6). This principle is the tendency to actualize our individual capacities, i.e., our nature in the world as much as is possible. This is the basic drive, the only drive by which the life of the organism is determined.

Psychologically disturbed people have a different principle. Disturbed people tend to preserve the existent state, because that is the only form of self-actualization possible. However, even disturbed people try to utilize their remaining capacities in the best way. Individuals with pathological conditions often demonstrate defective centering, in which some processes become detached or isolated from the total organism.

To be normal is to actualize your essential peculiarities, that is, to meet your adequate milieu and the tasks arising from it. Abnormality involves dangers to your existence and to the self-actualization of your self, and also involves defective responsiveness. People deal with psychological disturbance by shrinking their environment and often by defective centering (that is, poorer integration). Disturbed people may also occupy themselves with "substitute" performances.

The healthy person, then, continually has to come to terms with the environment, thereby experiencing minor catastrophic reactions and the accompanying anxiety. We find, therefore, tendencies both to avoid anxiety (such as the desire for order, norms, continuity, and homogeneity) and potentially to generate anxiety (such as the desire for growth and conquest of the world.) Conflict with the opposing forces of the environment is inevitable, and the healthy person faces and deals with the accompanying anxiety.

Goldstein disliked the notion that many drives exist. He prefers to focus upon his one proposed "need." Furthermore, he objected to the notion that drives have the goal of releasing tension (see Maslow's similar idea discussed in Chapter 3). These notions, he argued, are characteristic only of disturbed people. Healthy people have definite potentialities and the need to realize or actualize them.

Since the environment includes other people also seeking to actualize their potential, we may not be able to completely realize our own nature. Conflict and competition with others is unavoidable. People develop *habits* to cope with conditions imposed by the nonhuman environment, whereas *customs* are means of adaptation to the general conditions of life in a group.

The Unconscious

Goldstein reconceptualized the split between the conscious and the unconscious as simply a figure–ground dichotomy, in much the same way as Allport, discussed above. Processes in the unconscious are simply processes in the background—there because they do not fit into present behavior patterns. The processes can become conscious when they enter into present responses, typically because the individual is brought into a situation similar to that in which the processes originated. Goldstein preferred the term *nonconscious* and, for him, nonconscious processes included bodily processes (such as postures), inner experiences (such as feelings, moods, desires, needs, and attitudes), and forgotten events. Goldstein noted that his concept of the unconscious was very different from that of Freud.

Consciousness also had a special meaning for Goldstein. Consciousness involves experiencing ourselves as an object, equivalent to other objects, an abstract attitude. Conscious and nonconscious processes are integrated into a definite configuration. When we focus on one or the other, we are artificially isolating one aspect of the total behavior.

Goldstein suggested that a state exists similar to that described by Eastern philosophies, in which there is a feeling of unity comprising ourselves and the world, and in which subject–object experiences remain in the background. He called this state the *sphere of immediacy*.

Individual Differences

Goldstein was unwilling to classify people into types, but he did distinguish three common styles of human behavior: the thinker who focuses upon conscious processes; the poet who focuses on nonconscious attitudes, feelings, and moods; and the person of action who focuses on reacting to the milieu.

He noted that people have different rhythms for their performances, and may prefer different sensory modalities and concrete versus abstract approaches. People differ in their preferred performances—performances that correspond best to the capacities of the organism.

Discussion

Goldstein's holistic theory has much in common with that proposed by Angyal. However, Goldstein focused a great deal on the alternative theories that he opposed. As a result, he did not propose a detailed theory of his own for discussing personality, but left us with a general philosophical scheme and few specific concepts or examples. For example, to propose that all organisms have one overall need (that of self-actualization) does not permit a discussion of each person's individuality.

R. D. LAING

R. D. Laing (1967), an existential psychiatrist first discussed in Chapter 7, formulated a holistic theory of personality and applied it extensively to abnormal behavior. One of Laing's basic concepts is that of *experience*. He is concerned with how people experience the world (both internal events and external events).

The only information we receive is through our own experience. Therefore, we understand the experience of others only from inferences we make from our experience of their behavior. The study of the interaction of your own experience and that of others is called *social phenomenology*. Social phenomenology is the study of inter-experience.

Laing does not like the classification of experience into inner and outer (or perception versus imagination, etc.). He prefers to view perception, imagination, fantasy, reverie, dreams, memory, and so forth simply as different modalities of experience. Laing objects to seeing experience as *intra*psychic. Your psyche is your experience; your experience is your psyche. One is not inside the other.

People may be defined, in terms of experience, as the center of orientation of the objective universe and, in terms of behavior, as the origin of actions. Actions are a result of personal experience and, in turn, affect personal experience. The two most important aspects of people are the person as person (the mask or part being played) and the person as actual self. This division corresponds to the concepts of the real self and social self in Angyal's theory (see Chapter 7).

Laing notes that much human behavior is an attempt to eliminate experience. We forget both past experiences and experiences such as dreams. We are insensitive to our bodies. We fail to sense much of the environment. The psychoanalytic defense mechanisms are ways of eliminating experience and distorting experience. In these many ways we become alienated from our selves. Laing argues that, if our experience is lost or destroyed, then we lose our *selves*. (This emphasis on underawareness can also be found in the theory of Fritz Perls discussed later in this chapter.)

Experience is both active and passive (by which Laing seems to refer to something similar to Piaget's distinction between assimilation and accommodation). Furthermore, the construction we place upon events can be positive (desirable or acceptable) or negative (feared or not acceptable).

For Laing, the psychologically healthy person has recovered the wholeness of being human. Attempts to explain people by analyzing parts is fruitless. We start the road to psychological health in a shambles, without inner unity. The goal is to reconstitute our selves.

In talking of psychopathology, Laing does not have any use for the different psychiatric classifications. Madness is simply the result of our alienation from experience. The more severe forms of psychiatric disturbances, such as schizophrenia, represent refusals to adapt to this alienation. They are labels affixed by others to someone who refuses or is unable to adapt to the conforming, alienating pressures from society.

Although Laing dislikes the distinction between the inner and outer worlds of experience, he notes that psychotics have entered into an exploration of the inner world, unfortunately without a guide, and often confuse inner with outer realities. As a result, they lose their ability to function competently in ordinary relationships.

Laing also gives little credence to such dualities as mind/body, psyche/soma, psychological/physical, personality/self. All that a person is, is his *being*. Laing is especially opposed to treating humans as things. People who consider themselves to be robots, machinery, or things are typically seen as insane. Should not proponents of theories treating humans in that way also be considered insane?

The healthy person develops a sense of ontological security, a sense of presence in the world as a real, alive, whole and (in a temporal sense) continuous person. An ontologically secure person has a firm sense of his own reality/identity and of the reality/identity of others. The normal person has secrets and a need to confess. When normal people lie, they discover themselves irredeemably alone. This genuine privacy is the basis for genuine relationships. However, the schizophrenic feels both more exposed and more vulnerable to others and also more isolated. (Laing's description of the schizophrenic was presented in more detail in Chapter 7.)

Laing is much clearer about what he disapproves of in a potential theory than about what the theory should contain. Unfortunately, his refusal to break down his holistic concepts into component parts makes the development of his theory and the derivation of hypotheses from the theory difficult.

KURT LEWIN

Kurt Lewin (1935, 1936) stressed that the mind was a temporally extended whole and not a set of rigid connections of distinct pieces or elements. The mind is dynamic because forces in the mind and the environment are changed by the process of interaction. The whole is continuously changing under the influence of internal and external forces.

Because the mind is a unified whole, the proper questions of personality concern the structure of the whole, the interactions of *subwholes*, and the boundaries between subwholes. For example, subwholes may not have clear communication with one another. The communication may be weak or nonexistent. Without some segregation between subwholes, ordered action would be impossible. In addition, some subwholes may be considered "central" whereas others are "peripheral." The effect of subwholes on the person is primarily determined through the whole in which they are embedded. Clearly the concept of subwhole in Lewin's theory is analogous to Angyal's concept of subsystem (see Chapter 6) and the concept of subself introduced in Chapter 8.

Like most theorists in the early part of this century, Lewin was concerned with the energy behind psychological processes. He felt that psychical energies are always necessary for behaviors to occur. Every psychical event must have causal energies behind it.

The forces which control the course of the process remain without effect or simply do not arise when no psychical energies are present, when there exists no connection with tense psychical systems which keep the process in motion. (Lewin, 1935, pp. 50-51)

We discussed in Chapter 2 how energy concepts are no longer needed in modern theories of personality.

Behavior was seen by Lewin as typically leading to a reduction in tension, and so lowering tension levels is a determining factor of human behavior.

Tensions may be aroused by inner needs or by external objects (or by an interaction of the two). Objects that elicit tensions are said to possess a *valence*, and the forces from the environment that affect the person are called *field forces*. (This is probably where Angyal, see Chapter 6, derived the terms he chose for describing the biosphere as viewed from the object pole, that is, from the environmental perspective.) Objects have valences primarily because they are a means to satisfy a need. Valences in the environment and the needs of the individual are *correlative*.

Lewin also rephrased this by saying that psychical processes have a tendency toward equilibrium. The process changes, however, so that the system as a whole moves toward equilibrium, though part processes may go in opposite directions (c.f., Jung's concept of balance discussed in Chapter 8). Systems in equilibrium may also have residual tensions, as does a spring under tension. This requires subsystems with firm boundaries and actual segregation of the systems from their environment.

In both the person and the environment, Lewin distinguished between momentary situations and long-term dispositions. (For the field, he called these the *momentary situation* and the *milieu* respectively.) Psychological behavior is always a function of the momentary structure and state of both the environment and the person.

Field forces can be divided into driving forces (with positive or negative valences) and restraining forces (such as barriers). Three kinds of conflict can result from field forces: approach–approach, avoidance–avoidance, and approach–avoidance. Field forces in conflict increase the tension in the person.

The Mind

People differ in the number of subsystems in their mind, that is, the degree of differentiation. The child is less differentiated (or stratified) and has fewer subsystems than the adult. Second, the dynamic material of the subsystems may also be different. Subsystems can differ in fluidity and rigidity, for example, and systems can change with different amounts of ease (suddenly versus gradually; c.f., the discussion of set and shifting set in Berne's theory, discussed in Chapter 8). Children's subsystems are, on the whole, more fluid than those of adults. Third, the content of subsystems may differ. This may be crucially determined by life experiences. Finally, the subsystems may be relatively harmonious or in conflict.

Lewin distinguished between the realms of realistic and unreal behaviors in the mind. In the latter he included hopes, dreams, and fantasy. The unreal realm is dynamically a more fluid medium. Limits and barriers in it are less firm. The boundary between the self and the environment is also more fluid.

The *self* or *ego* was seen by Lewin as one subsystem of the whole. He saw this self as roughly equivalent to the conscious region of the mind.

Marked differences exist between people in the tempo, extent, and age limits of differentiation, as well as in the tempo and extent of the stiffening of psychical material. In the retarded, differentiation proceeds more slowly and ceases (or begins to decline) earlier. Individuals differ in which parts differentiate most (for example, intellectual versus non-intellectual parts) and in the functional significance of different parts (does a part play a primary or second- ary role in one's life?).

Very fluid systems will differentiate very easily momentarily. However, the slightest force will alter the structure so that development of a relatively per- manent differentiated structure is difficult. At the other extreme, functional rigidity with respect to changes also hinders differentiation. Lewin felt that it is possible that the rate of differentiation might be either an inherited predis- position or acquired as a result of life experiences.

Because the environment must be perceived in order for it to have an impact, the experienced environment can also be perceived as having a degree of differentiation. Lewin felt that this degree of differentiation was related to the degree of differentiation of the person. (Note that Angyal, as discussed in Chapter 6, implies that this differentiation actually exists in the environment, whereas Lewin sees the differentiation as being in our perception of the envi- ronment.)

In general, Lewin argued that a system is more strongly unified if it contains fewer parts or subsystems, if the subsystems are less separated from one another, if the structural arrangement of the subsystems promotes unification (for example, if each subsystem interacts with every other subsystem rather than in a linear chain), and if the whole system is more strongly separated from the environment. States of great inner tension also bring about unification of the mind.

A person's structure remains relatively constant over a long period of time. But sudden changes can occur, for example, when a person falls in love or undergoes a religious conversion. Parts of the system can also separate them- selves off and develop relatively independently. This sometimes occurs in healthy people, but more often in the mentally ill.

Lewin suggested that newly developed subsystems have less firm boundaries than older subsystems. Thus, under external stimulation, a more unified re- action occurs. Changes in the fluidity of the system caused by factors such as fatigue have a similar effect.

Life Space

Lewin (1936) defined the concept of psychological *life space* as "the totality of facts which determine the behavior of in individual at a certain moment" (Lewin, 1936, p. 12). Lewin sometimes used the word "events" in place of "facts" in the above definition. The life space includes the person himself and psychological "objects," that is, the perceived environment. It includes the physical environment and any object that is important to the individual. Thus, the life space is a subjective concept, namely, how the world is perceived by the individual. Life space includes somatic processes, the physical world as it affects the person's momentary situation, social facts as the person perceives them, and cognitive processes (or conceptual facts). The principle processes in the person are *needs* and in the life space are *valences*.

Lewin recognized that many forces acting on the person from the environ- ment are a result of the individual's *perception* of something. However, other forces exist (for example, floods or tornadoes) that influence the person regardless of how they are perceived (although our perception of the event may add other influences), and these are not part of the psychological life space.

Applications

The child and the adult. For the child, as compared to the adult, the real and unreal systems are less differentiated. Furthermore, the boundary between the self and the environment is less well-defined. The child, being less differentiated, is a dynamic unity to a greater extent than the adult. However, the less well-defined boundary between the self and the environment means that the child is affected more by field forces.

Retarded individuals. The mentally retarded person is also less differentiated. Furthermore, the subsystems are less able to be dynamically rearranged, that is, they are more rigid. Retarded people have more unified, internally undifferentiated systems that, in so far as they are separated, are separated completely (by stronger and more rigid boundaries). In the second respect, Lewin felt that the retarded show extreme characteristics, that is, a paucity of continuously graded transitions between absolute separation and absolute connection between the subsystems.

Valences seem to be stronger in retarded people, which puts them more at the mercy of the momentary situation and more sensitive to distractions. The lack of differentiation makes dissimulation harder for them.

Lewin saw insight as a change in the relations between subparts in the field, an ability to restructure one's perception of the field. Retarded individuals are less able to achieve these restructurings. In addition, they have less development of the unreal system, leading to lowered imaginativeness and increased concreteness of thinking.

Other children, labeled as "problem children" by Lewin, are at the other extreme of retarded children, because they have a more fluid organization. Subsystems are less separated, indicating a closer connection between central and peripheral parts and permitting central parts to have a greater effect on external behavior. However, like retarded children, problem children are less differentiated than the normal child, so that their central parts are "less deep," resulting in superficial expressions.

Individuals with senile dementia. The change from plasticity to firmness in the boundaries of the subsystems leads in old age to rigidity, lack of mobility, and inelasticity, i.e., a progressive stiffening of the system's material properties. Also, an increasing differentiation of the total person occurs. If stiffening occurs faster and differentiation occurs more slowly, then intellectual abilities will decrease with age. Furthermore, with increasing age, an impoverishment of structure may occur, a loss of part systems, which makes intellectual decline even more marked.

Discussion

Interestingly, Lewin has had more influence on social psychology than on theories of personality, probably because many of his students went on to work in that particular field. Nevertheless, it can be seen that Lewin promoted a holistic theory of personality, and he extended his theory to individuals, such as the retarded and the senile, that other theorists have neglected. Thus, Lewin's ideas show how the range of applicability of a holistic theory can be broadened.

KARL MENNINGER

Karl Menninger (Menninger, Mayman, & Pruyser, 1967) began his theory by defining his concept of mental illness. He rejected all of the classification schemes proposed over the centuries for mental illness and instead suggested that a holistic, humanistic, and unitary concept of mental illness was appropriate. All mental illnesses are essentially the same in quality and differ only in quantity. Mental illness is best viewed as a personality dysfunction and as an impairment in living. People are not afflicted with psychiatric "diseases," but rather are making awkward and expensive maneuvers to maintain themselves. Mental illness is a process in flux, rather than a motley collection of bizarre entities.

Menninger then described the concepts necessary for a theory of personality to give his concept of mental illness a sound basis.

Adaptation and Balance

The organism has to make continuous adaptations to changes in the internal and external conditions. Much of the time, the organism can make these adjustments and restore itself to its initial state. But sometimes the organism has pre-existing weaknesses that make adaptation difficult. Perhaps the scars of previous efforts have weakened it, or the internal and external conditions are of such a magnitude that restoration is impossible. Then comes a crisis— a state of emergency—and special maneuvers are initiated. There is an imbalance, an organismic disequilibrium. The injury suffered, and the reactions to both this injury and the set of stressors, constitute the mental illness.

Looking at the interaction between the organism and the environment, the goal is mutual coexistence, to get things from each other and to get along. When both the individual and the environment are satisfied, there is adjustment (equilibrium). When either (or both) is depleted or injured, there is no adjustment. People interact with the environment, give to it, take from it, alter it and are altered by it.

The individual maintains an equilibrium with the environment by means of symbols, feelings, gestures, thoughts, and acts. There is reciprocity and integration of the same kind that takes place in physiological *homeostasis*.

Organization

Organisms maintain a flexible balance internally between the different parts, as well as the previously mentioned balance with the environment, the *vital balance*. The organism maintains its own uniqueness and integrity, despite variations, both internal and external. It must be organized, but capable of changing its internal organization and level of operation. The organism endeavors to maintain a relatively constant inner and outer environment by correcting for upsetting eventualities. Threats of radical change mobilize and direct energies to retard further changes and to restore the initial state.

Occasionally, homeostasis at one level seems to fail. Certain long-term processes, such as growth, maturation, and decline, seem to argue against homeostasis. Organisms effect change, even initiating some of the very disturbances that upset the organism. Then again, the different homeostatic processes may conflict. Or there may be conflict between the regulated interaction with the environment and the regulated internal processes. There is a hierarchy of levels in the organism and, although each is regulated homeostatically, there is also an overall homeostatic tendency. Thus, occasionally heterostasis, a progressive moving away from the status quo, occurs, a search for new and unsettled states.

Servo-Mechanisms

Menninger also made use of the notion of cybernetic feedback devices, which help monitor conditions in an organism and signal the need for maneuvers to restore the organism to its previous state. He noted that often cybernetic restoration does not result in a smooth return, but rather corrective overactivity that may overdo (or underdo) the job, overshooting or undershooting the mark, leading to an oscillatory process.

Open Systems

The living organism is an open system. It exchanges energy with its environment; its components are in flux; it maintains itself as a whole; and it changes to different levels of organization as necessary (for example, during growth). It maintains a constancy best described as a *steady state*. This steady state is not static. The parts are in constant flux, with a perpetual intake and expenditure of energy, and the state of rest is never reached.

Content of the Mind

In describing the content of the mind, Menninger, on the whole, followed Freud. He placed most stress on the ego, that part of the mind that experiences, perceives, reflects, suffers, and decides. The ego carries out most of the self-regulatory processes. The ego is an advanced subsystem, a product of differentiation, and a means to the ends of constancy maintenance, adaptation, self-regulation, self-preservation, growth, and procreation. It is fairly autonomous.

Menninger does not talk of the id subsystem, but rather of instincts. The instinctual functions and ego functions represent different levels of organization and activity, according to Menninger, which interact with each other for the sake of the whole. The ego is the controlling agency, however, and has to

Table 9.1 Different terms for opposing forces

Opposing forces		Source
life	death	
love	hate	
anabolism	katabolism	
constructiveness	destructiveness	
good	evil	Mani
yang	yin	ancient China
Eros	Neikos	Empedocles
Eros	Thanatos	Freud
libido	mortido	Federn
forces of light	darkness	Zoroaster (essences)
assimilation	accommodation	Piaget
synthesis	disintegration	Spencer
diastole	systole	Harvey; Goethe

Adapted from Menninger, Marman, & Pruyser, 1967, p. 116.

mediate and manage the instincts (and the physiological processes as well). The ego is the guardian of the vital balance.

Menninger also accepted Freud's proposal of two drives, or sources of energy, two opposing tendencies. There is a creative, synthesizing, reproductive, erotic trend, and a destructive, regressive, disintegrative trend—what Freud called the life and death instincts, respectively. Menninger noted that this dichotomy has been a common proposal (Table 9.1).

"Going to Pieces"

What happens when the system maintenance goes awry? The ego makes efforts to restore the system to its former state. The success depends upon constitutional predispositions, previous battles and the extent of the threat to the organism's integrity.

To describe the ego's efforts to control disturbances considerably out of the ordinary in degree, Menninger proposed using the following terms: *dysfunctions, dyscontrol,* and *dysorganization.* Increasing dysfunction, dyscontrol, and dysorganization can be identified in a series of hierarchical levels, each one reflecting a stage of greater impairment of control and organization.

The ego can make a series of maneuvers of increasing effort:

everyday coping devices (e.g., crying, sleeping, or dreaming)
first-order dysfunctions (symptoms of stress; nervousness)
second-order dysfunctions (neurotic reactions)
third-order dysfunctions (episodic dyscontrol)
fourth-order dysfunctions (psychotic reactions)
fifth-order dysfunctions (malignant anxiety and depression/suicide)

Discussion

Menninger was a psychiatrist, and has been commonly viewed as a psychoanalytically inclined theorist. However, his writings on the mind clearly show that he had moved far from a simple psychoanalytic position to a more holistic perspective. His notion of the unitary and global nature of psychological disturbance is very similar to the views of Andras Angyal. However, whereas Angyal made few proposals about the content of the mind, Menninger adopted a more traditional psychoanalytic viewpoint, using the concepts of ego, id, and superego and the notion of life and death instincts.

HENRY MURRAY

Henry Murray never proposed a theory of personality in the sense that other theorists have. Rather, he took the theories proposed by others and formed an amalgam of them, so that his writings are somewhat like an introduction to human behavior written in general terms.

Murray (1959) listed those disciplines and theorists that influenced his theory of personality. From Freud, Murray adopted the division of psychological material into conscious and unconscious parts and a belief in the importance of early experiences for the development of personality. He also found the organismic, holistic, or molar conceptions of personality useful, although not rejecting completely the usefulness of focusing at times on the elements that make up the whole. Murray's preference was to conceptualize the organization of the parts as hierarchical systems with vertical integrations of superordinate and subordinate parts. Murray's analyses of the elements focused mainly upon needs and subneeds (subordinate components of a larger system of *need-aims*), and *dispositions* (sentiments, interests, attitudes, and evaluations).

Murray also emphasized the distinction between the needs of the individual and the influence of the environment. The forces of the environment were called the *alpha press*; the forces of the environment as perceived by the subject were called the *beta press*. The beta press is a better predictor of a person's behavior than is the alpha press. Interestingly, Murray changed Freud's definition of cathexis from a property of the mind to a property of the environment. He defined *cathexis* as the disposition-evoking capacity of any kind of event, that is the capacity of an event in the environment to evoke attention, evaluation, and behavior.

Murray was interested in detailing inventories of the content of some of the psychological processes. For example, he listed and devised ways of measuring some fundamental needs of humans. First, he proposed that the system of personality could be seen as composed of four subsystems, involving (a) a psychosomatic system (needs and activities concerned with the growth and welfare of the body), (b) a psychosexual system (needs and activities concerned with erotic love), (c) a psychosocial system (needs and activities concerned with non-erotic social reciprocations), and (d) a psychorepresentational system (cognitive needs associated with the above systems). The personality system is composed of these systems and their subsystems and questions about behavior concern the allocation of energy to these various component systems and subsystems. Murray was primarily concerned with particular *regnancies*, the needs, and he proposed classifications of these needs and of the environmental forces acting upon the individual (press). In Chapter 3, we mentioned this classification and that later psychologists have sometimes adopted it as the basis for their psychological tests.

In an early statement of his theory, Murray (1938) stressed the wholeness of humans at birth, after which they begin to differentiate into parts. The whole and the parts are mutually related and cannot be understood separately. Furthermore, there is a temporal unity. The history of the person is the person. Eventually, conflict between the parts occurs and, with increasing age, conflict resolution—synthesis and creative integration back into a unified whole again. Murray proposed that psychic events or processes that govern our behavior at each moment in time, be called regnant processes or *regnancies*. Regnancies may be conscious or unconscious.

Sequences in which press are followed by needs, thereby resulting in behavior (or in Murray's terminology *actones*), were called *thema*. A succession of such episodes is called a *complex thema*. If a person has characteristic modes of behavior, in which certain press result in characteristic needs and characteristic behaviors, Murray referred to this as a *need integrate* or *complex*. Behaviors that result from internal needs are *proactive*, whereas those that result from external press are *reactive*.

Discussion

Murray introduced few new concepts and no new integration of the concepts previously proposed. Rather, Murray accepted the views of others and tried to combine all of these ideas to give a balanced view of human behavior. However, his views provide a good example of the holistic point of view.

TALCOTT PARSONS

Talcott Parsons (1959, 1966), a sociologist, has been concerned with human behavior or the *human action system*, for which he has proposed an analysis called a *general theory of action*. The human action system is comprised of four subsystems: the cultural system, the social system, the psychological system, and the physiological system.

1. Cultural systems are concerned with pattern maintenance. The cultural system defines and maintains the meanings of the parts of the system and transmits these systematically patterned meanings from one person to another.

2. Social systems are concerned with the integration of the parts of the system. As a sociologist, Parsons was especially concerned with social systems and, in particular, with one type of social system—societies.
3. Psychological systems are concerned with the organization of the individual's behavior (primarily centered around goal attainment). In particular, the total behavior system of a living organism was called the *personality*.
4. Finally, the organism possesses a physiologically functioning system that is concerned with adaptation to the environment.

These four subsystems are arranged in order of organization and control. The cultural system controls the social system, which in turn controls the psychological system, and so on. Parsons called this control *cybernetic*, by which he meant that systems high in information and low in energy regulate systems lower in information but higher in energy (much as switches control machines, or genes control cell metabolism). The cultural system is also more organized than the social system, and so on. In contrast, the lower systems impose conditions upon the higher systems, and set limitations on human behavior. The four subsystems are also arranged in the reverse order from which they appear in the phylogenetic scale (evolutionary development) and ontogenetically (temporal development of a system).

As a systems theorist, Parsons was sympathetic to an analysis of subsystems. For example, he noted that a society contains many subsystems: local communities, schools, business firms, and kinship units.

General Systems

All systems are concerned with pattern maintenance, integration, goal attainment, and adaptation. Goal attainment and adaptation are concerned with the relations between the system and situations external to it. Pattern maintenance and integration are concerned with problems internal to the system. The component parts of systems have two properties: value orientation and potency. *Value orientation* refers to the meaning or function of the part, whereas *potency* refers to its relative degree of importance in determining outcomes. Typically, the parts of a system can be differentiated in a rank order of relative potency.

Systems interact with the environment. Maintenance of their distinctive intrasystem pattern, rather than assimilating into the patterning of the extrasystem situation, is a critical criterion for evaluating systems. How well the system is functioning is also an important issue. (How well adapted is it? How integrated is it?)

Social Systems

A society for Parsons is a self-sufficient social system. It is self-sufficient with respect to reality, cultural systems, psychological systems, physiological systems, and the physical–organic environment.

The social system of the society provides a patterned normative order, with statuses, rights, and obligations. The cultural system provides legitimation of the society's normative order (typically grounded in religion, arts, and sciences). The psychological system requires that the society teaches, develops, and maintains the motivation for its members to participate in the society, that is, the society must socialize its members.

Parsons felt that as societies developed from primitive to modern they became more differentiated social systems. They developed subsystems and sub-subsystems. The functions of each subsystem become increasingly specific. Work is more productive when conducted in a setting other than the family (for example, in a factory). So family and work split from each other. Pluralism of roles develops, and problems in integration occur. The cultural pattern of values must incorporate the modified society and, therefore, becomes more general.

In primitive societies, only a low level of differentiation between the four systems of action—cultural, social, psychological, and physiological—exists. The first development is typically that the cultural/social systems differentiate—individual autonomy versus collective action. In a primitive society, the actions systems are undifferentiated, and little differentiation exists between the four systems of action. In archaic societies (such as ancient Egypt), primitive religious systems appeared. In some advanced intermediate societies (such as India), primitive religious systems developed into historical religions with philosophical levels of generalization and systematization. However, in these intermediate societies, the cultural systems often failed to include the lower classes, whereas in advanced societies the cultural systems extended to include them.

Parsons divided society into three subsystems, each concerned with interaction with one of the three other systems (cultural, psychological, and physiological). The social system has to interact with the cultural system, so the cultural patterns of meaning become institutionalized (in the Catholic Church, for example.) The social system organizes its interaction with the psychological system by means of political systems (the organization of collective action for attaining collective goals). And finally, the social system interacts with the physiological system by means of economic systems.

The Psychological System

Psychological systems can be analyzed in terms of two sets of processes, those involving relations with external situations and those involving the relation of the component parts with one another. The components of psychological systems are needs and dispositions to act. Parsons noted that these need/dispositions have both emotional (or "cathectic") qualities and cognitive qualities. (Parsons also discussed roles as possible units for an analysis of psychological systems.) In his analysis of the psychological system, Parsons analyzed the relationship between the psychological system and the physiological system, objects in the environment (primarily people), and cultural systems. For ex-

---

A SYSTEM PRINCIPLE THAT CHANGES WITH AGE

Many of the theorists reviewed in this book have searched for one system principle that would cover all people. Angyal (Chapter 6) chose a double trend, the trends toward autonomy and homonomy. Lecky (Chapter 5) chose self-consistency, a principle that motivated people to achieve consistency between themselves and the environment and within themselves.

Parsons (1966) noted that societies are defined and maintained by a cultural system principle. Primitive societies, he argued, have a poor, almost nonexistent cultural system. In archaic societies, such as ancient Egypt, a cosmological religion developed that served as a rudimentary cultural system. In advanced intermediate societies, such as ancient India, the religion became an historic one with philosophical levels of generalization and systematization, and thus a truly cultural system. However, these cultural systems were typically reserved for the elite, and the lower classes remained unaffected by the cultural system. In modern societies, the cultural system extends to all of the population.

Lester (1984) noted that Parsons' general ideas could be extended to humans. Parsons' theories postulate that, as societies develop, the system principle changes. Perhaps as humans develop, their system principles also change? The system principle for a child need not necessarily be the same system principle as for an adult. Maslow's hierarchy of needs (see Chapter 3) suggests that children are dominated by different needs than adults (for example, physiological needs versus esteem needs), and so the corresponding system principles may differ. Even among adults, the level of psychological development (perhaps developmental stage—see Chapter 3) may affect the particular system principle in operation.

---

ample, cultural systems legitimize the behavior of the psychological system, by providing rationales. In return, the psychological system provides a motivational commitment to the cultural system. The psychological system understands and accepts the cultural guidelines.

For his internal analysis of the psychological system, Parsons deviated from a systems approach. He took the four problems that systems analysis must consider—pattern maintenance, integration, goal attainment, and adaptation—and explored the implications for a personality of each possible ranking pattern of these four problems, giving 24 possible orders for ranking these four problems.

Discussion

Parsons was a systems theorist and, therefore, his theories are relevant to the development of a systems conception of personality. The particular systems analysis proposed by Parsons for personality has little relevance for intrapsychic theories of personality. However, the overall scheme that Parsons proposed in his general theory of action has important implications for systems theories of personality. Problems of pattern maintenance (that is, the system principle and its relevance for the personality), the integration of the system, the adaptation of the system to the environment, and goal attainment are critical problems that systems theories of personality must address. Parsons' analysis of these problems for societies provides a stimulating analogy for the present task.

FREDERICK PERLS

Frederick (Fritz) Perls developed a system of psychotherapy called *gestalt therapy*, for which a theory of personality is his theoretical basis. Perls saw himself as firmly rooted in the concepts of gestalt psychology current in America in the 1930s. Gestalt psychology emphasized that psychological processes were an organized whole. This organized whole was made up of several parts, but the properties of the whole were more than the sum of the properties of the component parts. A favorite analogy of gestalt psychologists was that water is made up of hydrogen and oxygen, but its properties were very different from those of the two elements separately. The theoretical position behind this analogy permeates Perls' ideas on human behavior.

Perls (Perls, Hefferline, & Goodman, 1951) focused upon the interaction between the organism and the environment. Organisms live by maintaining the difference between themselves and the environment. They assimilate parts of the environment and reject others, and grow, therefore, at the expense of the environment. The parts that are assimilated are always novel; therefore, assimilation involves creative adjustments by the organism.

Whenever the person and the environment interact, there is *contact*. This contact is mutual. The person can be seen as the agent in this, or the environment can be seen as the agent, and so Perls refers to the contact boundary as a *field* and as a *mutual interaction*. In this, Perls' notion is very similar to the proposal of the biosphere by Andras Angyal (see Chapter 6).

Therapy is concerned with analyzing the structure of the actual experience of the contact. The therapist is not concerned with what is being experienced, but on how it is being experienced; not on what the person says, but how he says it. The goal is to heighten the contact and the awareness of the person.

As people grow and assimilate new experiences they have to make creative integrations of new material with old material. This often involves destroying the status quo—the former ways of perceiving the world. The person aims for a better integration of all the material, not a mere reshuffling of the components. The person finds and remakes himself. This process may easily arouse fear and anxiety: it is scary to change one's set habits if the new material demands that you do. The psychologically healthy person does not shrink from that task, but the neurotic avoids restructuring his perceptions and habits. Here, Perls is proposing views similar to those of George Kelly (see Chapter 4).

The *self* is your system of contacts with the environment at any time. The healthy person identifies with his self; the unhealthy person is alienated from his self. The unhealthy person tries to conquer his own spontaneity, and limit his assimilations. The set of identifications and alienations one has is called one's *ego*.

Because therapy aims to increase the contact between the person and the environment, therapy works on the ego. The goal is to train the ego by making it experiment with awareness—to make it more aware of the environment and of the body of the person. Once the ego has its senses revived and is making better contact, therapy is finished; the patient can take over from the therapist.

Neurotics typically are underaware. They are not fully aware of what they are seeing or of what their body is experiencing (*perception* and *proprioception*). They achieve this underawareness by blocking out of awareness certain inputs, and by creating and focusing on distracting inputs. For example, they may deliberately tighten and tense muscles. They may reject parts of their experience. The psychosomatic patient, for example, labels his body as "not me." His body becomes a problem to him. He suffers from asthma or ulcers. Yet he himself causes these problems. His symptoms are him. Rigid behavior and compulsions also serve to restrict the awareness of the patient.

The role of the therapeutic situation is to provide the patient with safe opportunities to experiment with opening up the patient's awareness. Perls was aware that the major difficulty is releasing the patient's healthy power of creative adjustments, without having him mimic the therapist's conception of reality. The aim is growth, not correction. Can society tolerate people regulating themselves with less regard for societal norms and values? Perls feels that society can tolerate more self-regulation than occurs at present.

The therapeutic situation is safe. The patient can experiment with low levels of anxiety. The patient does not flee from the anxiety, but remains in control of both the anxiety and his responses to it. The role of the therapist is to increase the anxiety of the patient while keeping the situation controllable.

Perls believed that what takes place within the person is good. The body can be trusted to be self-regulating. So, for example, if the patient has some inner conflicts, the therapist should not try to eliminate these conflicts. Conflict is a means of growth. The therapist's task is to make the patient aware of the conflicts so that they may feed on environmental material and come to a crisis point. The sharper a conflict, the greater the battle, and the more likely the outcome or solution will be a good one. Working through conflicts enables people to grow. The neurotic has become neurotic partly by trying to resolve the conflicts too quickly.

Many conflicts stem from early situations that the patient left unfinished, that is, unresolved. They affect present behavior because the patient repeatedly tries to finish the situation in current situations, and so energy is diverted from growth-producing activity. One task of therapy is to find these unfinished situations and try to help the person resolve them. Once the unfinished situation is completed, the dominance of past traumas will be lessened.

If you can experience a conflict, you must remember that both sides of the conflict are you. The person must not label one part of the self as "me" and the other part as "not me." Both must be labeled "me" and must eventually be synthesized into a unified whole.

Perls defined three major neurotic mechanisms.

1. *Retroflection* is redirecting activity inwards, substituting oneself for the environment as the target for behavior. Instead of attacking someone else, you direct the anger inwards on yourself and become depressed.

2. *Introjection* is taking in material from the environment but not assimilating it as a genuine part of yourself.
3. *Projection* occurs when you do not experience your own traits, attitudes, feelings, or behaviors as your own, but attribute them to other people in the environment who are then seen as directing them toward yourself.

Discussion

Perls accepted many psychoanalytic ideas, but placed more emphasis on holistic considerations. Furthermore, in his emphasis on conflict and divisions in the psychic structures, Perls' notions are similar to those of Jung.

CONCLUSIONS

Although the theories presented in this chapter are not major innovations in the field, they do provide some alternative terms to those reviewed earlier in this volume, with definitions that have different connotations. Thus, some readers may prefer these terms and theories to others. The theories presented here also extend the major theories to some neglected areas and topics. The usefulness of these alternative theories is illustrated by the different ways in which students who have been trained in these theories have moved on, some to become personality or social psychological researchers, others to become psychotherapists.

Therefore, the theories presented in this chapter provide alternatives to the three major theories presented in this volume, despite the fact that they are not as extensive as nor radically different from those of Freud, Kelly, and Angyal. The reader is not left to ponder some 20 or more different theories of personality, but instead to consider three complex and well-described theories, complemented by interesting alternative phrasings and supplemental ideas provided by others. Perhaps the coming years will produce a theorist who integrates the basic theories and the supplemental ideas reviewed here into a new and comprehensive holistic theory of the structure of the mind.

IV

CONCLUSIONS

10

Conclusions

This chapter reviews the goals of the book and explores to what extent they were met. This book focused on the intrapsychic theories of personality, that is, those theories that propose hypothetical constructs for the mind in order to explain certain aspects human behavior: why individuals behave similarly to one another in some ways yet differently in other ways, and why individuals behave consistently over time.

CHOICE OF THE SEMINAL THEORISTS

To do this I chose three major theories—Freud's psychoanalytic theory, George Kelly's personal construct theory, and Andras Angyal's holistic theory. This set of choices has several implications. First, I cast Freud's psychoanalytic theory as a theory of motivation, Kelly's personal construct theory as a theory of cognition, and I noted that there was no comprehensive theory of personality based on emotions. This categorization is, of course, open to question. Psychoanalytic theory does address some issues of cognition, and both psychoanalytic and personal construct theories do discuss emotions. Other scholars might categorize these two theories differently, and they might argue that some theorist has proposed a theory of personality based on emotions.

Second, I claimed that the theories of Freud, Kelly, and Angyal were the most comprehensive intrapsychic theories in each of their respective viewpoints—motivational, cognitive, and holistic. Obviously, others may think differently. After reading the original works of other theorists whose views are discussed in this volume, I decided that their concepts and propositions are not as extensive as those of Freud, Kelly, and Angyal. Some scholars might prefer another theorist as the seminal holistic theorist; indeed, Angyal's theory is rarely presented in modern textbooks. However, none of the theorists discussed in Chapter 9, for example, Allport, Goldstein, Laing, Lewin, Menninger, Murray, Parsons, and Perls, are routinely presented in modern textbooks of personality either, nor are those those theorists discussed in Chapters 7 and 8. Goldstein, Lewin, and Murray have often been omitted from textbooks on personality in recent years; Laing and Menninger are mentioned primarily in textbooks on abnormal psychology for their writings on psychiatric disorder; Perls is covered only in textbooks on theories of counseling for his development of gestalt therapy; Parsons, as a sociologist, is rarely covered in psychology textbooks; whereas Allport is seen as a simple trait theorist with similarities to other trait theorists, such as Raymond Cattell and Hans Eysenck, and the holistic aspects of his writings ignored. Thus, none of these seem to be rivals to Angyal; this is particularly clear once one examines the range of hypothetical constructs and descriptive terms introduced by each theorist.

Thus, I remain convinced that I have chosen the three most comprehensive theories, but I will enthusiastically read an alternative proposal if such a book appears.

NEGLECT OF HOLISTIC VIEWPOINTS

A striking feature of this book is the large set of holistic theorists. Indeed, whereas modifications and alternatives to Freud and Kelly's theories could be covered in one chapter each, three chapters were needed to cover alternative holistic viewpoints. The majority of theorists seem to be holistic and, indeed, holistic elements can be found in the theories of Freud and Kelly also.

The holistic aspects of personality theorists have often been neglected by textbooks writers. This may be because holistic theories are out of fashion, but it may also be that there was no major holistic theorist around whom to orient other holistic theorists. Perhaps a more detailed examination of Angyal's theory by scholars would convince them that Angyal provides this comprehensive framework.

ADDITIONAL CONCEPTS

Another claim I made in this book was that the theories of Freud, Kelly, and Angyal contained almost all of the major ideas relevant to intrapsychic theories of personality, although others may have proposed these ideas earlier. For example, Prescott Lecky (Chapter 5) published his book before Kelly published his. Others may have used terms that have proved more acceptable to other psychologists. For example, Rogers' terms involving conditions of worth and the discrepancy between these and the real self (Chapter 7) have found much more acceptance than Angyal's "pattern of vicarious living." I noted that other theorists may have presented the ideas in a form more suitable for generating research. For example, Festinger's concept of cognitive dissonance (Chapter 5) has generated much more research than Kelly's concept of hostility. Others have applied the ideas to other aspects of human behavior neglected by Freud, Kelly, and Angyal. For example, Lewin applied holistic concepts to those with retardation and senile dementia (Chapter 9), whereas Laing applied what is essentially Angyal's pattern of vicarious living to schizophrenics (Chapter 7). Furthermore, the writings of others sometimes serve to provide good examples of the more abstract elements of Freud, Kelly, and Angyal, and this was particularly true for Jung's and Berne's examples of Angyalian subsystems (Chapter 8)

I claimed that few new ideas have been proposed above and beyond those in Freud, Kelly, and Angyal, and I have endeavored to indicate the congruence between the concepts proposed by these three and those proposed by others. However, as noted in Chapter 8, Jung's notion that subsystems in the mind are paired up such that the two members of each pair counterbalance each other in their characteristics is an idea not found in other theories of personality. This, to my mind, is an innovative and useful proposition.

HOW MANY THEORIES OF PERSONALITY ARE THERE?

Finally, I mentioned my confusion as a student long ago in finding that there were dozens of theories of personality. To someone coming from the natural sciences in which theories are less abundant, this number seemed excessive. I have tried to show that these dozens of theories of personality are not really separate and different theories competing to explain the same phenomena, but rather can be reduced to three basic theories. Indeed, I have discussed the ideas of at least 38 theorists in this brief volume, and I find that all these ideas could be contained in the theories of Freud, Kelly, and Angyal—after modification. The last point is critical because the three basic theories do need to be modified. Obviously, Freud, Kelly, and Angyal themselves were unable to include the modifications and extensions proposed by others. The present generation of scholars must do so. Writers of college textbooks generally do not do this because they are more concerned with presenting the theories as distinct entities. Researchers await a new theorist who will assimilate the old theories and present an integrated theory incorporating previous concepts and propositions. A cynical colleague of mine once said that such a task requires the services of someone in marketing because the ideas will not be new ones but merely old ones presented in new packaging.

References

Adams-Webber, J. R. (1970). Actual structure and potential chaos. In D. Bannister (Ed.), *Perspectives in personal construct theory* (pp. 31–46). London: Academic Press.

Adams-Webber, J. R. (1979). *Personal construct theory*. Chichester, England: Wiley.

Allison, R., & Schwartz, T. (1980). *Minds in many pieces*. New York: Rawson-Wade.

Allport, G. W. (1937). *Personality*. New York: Holt.

Allport, G. W. (1955). *Becoming*. New Haven, CT: Yale University.

Allport, G. W. (1961). *Pattern and growth in personality*. New York: Holt, Rinehart & Winston.

Angyal, A. (1941). *Foundations for a science of personality*. New York: Commonwealth Fund.

Angyal, A. (1965). *Neurosis and treatment: A holistic theory*. New York: Wiley.

Assagoli, R. (1975). *Psychosynthesis*. London: Turnstone.

Atwood, G. E., & Tomkins, S. S. (1976). On the subjectivity of personality theory. *Journal of the History of the Behavioral Sciences, 12*, 166–177.

Berlyne, D. (1960). *Conflict, arousal and curiosity*. New York: McGraw-Hill.

Berne, E. (1961). *Transactional analysis in psychotherapy*. New York: Grove.

Berne, E. (1964). *Games people play*. New York: Grove Press.

Bettelheim, B. (1982). Reflections: Freud and the soul. *New Yorker, 58*(2), 52–93.

Borst, S. R., & Noam, G. G. (1993). Developmental psychopathology in suicidal and nonsuicidal adolescent girls. *Journal of the American Academy of Child and Adolescent Psychiatry, 32*, 501–508.

Boulding, K. E. (1968). *The organizational revolution*. Chicago: Quadrangle.

Bruner, J. S. (1956). A cognitive theory of personality. *Contemporary Psychology, 1*, 355–356.

Caputi, J. (1987). *The age of sex crime*. Bowling Green, OH: Bowling Green State University Press.

Cattell, R. B. (1948). Concepts and methods in the measurement of group syntality. *Psychological Review, 55*, 48–63.

Chapanis, N. P., & Chapanis, A. (1964). Cognitive dissonance. *Psychological Bulletin*, 61, 1–22.

Chomsky, N. (1975). *The logical structure of linguistic theory*. New York: Plenum.

Cofer, C. N., & Appley, M. H. (1964). *Motivation: Theory and research*. New York: Wiley.

Cromwell, R. L., & Caldwell, D. F. (1962). A comparison of ratings based on personal constructs of self and others. *Journal of Clinical Psychology, 18,* 43–46.

Davidson, D. (1985). Deception and division. In J. Elster (Ed.), *The multiple self* (pp. 79–92). New York: Cambridge University Press.

Dennett, D. C. (1978). *Brainstorms.* Brighton: Harvester.

de Sousa, R. (1976). Rational homunculi. In A. O. Rorty (Ed.), *The identities of persons.* Berkeley, CA: University of California.

Dundes, A. (1978). Into the endzone for a touchdown. *Western Folklore, 37,* 75–88.

Ehrlich, D., Guttman, I., Schönbach, P., & Mills, J. (1957). Postdecision exposure to relevant information. *Journal of Abnormal and Social Psychology, 54,* 98–102.

Elster, J. (1985). Introduction. In J. Elster (Ed.), *The multiple self* (pp. 1–34). New York: Cambridge University Press.

Erikson, E. H. (1950). *Childhood and society.* New York: Norton.

Erikson, E. (1968). *Identity: Youth and crisis.* New York: Norton.

Eysenck, H. J. (1967). *The biological basis of personality.* Springfield, IL: Charles C Thomas.

Eysenck, S. B. G., Eysenck, H. J., & Barrett, P. (1985). A revised version of the psychoticism scale. *Personality and Individual Differences, 6,* 21–29.

Fairbairn, W. R. D. (1954). *An object-relations theory of the personality.* New York: Basic Books.

Federn, P. (1952). *Ego psychology and the psychoses.* New York: Basic.

Festinger, L. (1957). *A theory of cognitive dissonance.* Palo Alto: Stanford University Press.

Fiske, D. W., & Maddi, S. R. (1961). *Functions of varied experience.* Homewood, IL: Dorsey.

Flavell, J. H. (1963). *The developmental psychology of Jean Piaget.* New York: Van Nostrand Reinhold.

Football as erotic ritual. (1978, November 13) *Time,* p. 112.

Frankl, V. (1963). *Man's search for meaning.* New York: Pocket Books.

Freud, S. (1933). *New introductory lectures on psychoanalysis.* New York: Norton.

Gay, P. (1988). *Freud.* New York: Norton.

Goldstein, K. (1963a). *The organism.* Boston: Beacon.

Goldstein, K. (1963b). *Human nature in the light of psychopathology.* New York: Schocken.

Gough, H. G. (1960). Theory and measurement of socialization. *Journal of Consulting Psychology, 24,* 23–30.

Gray, P. (1993, November 29). The assault on Freud. *Time, 142,* 46–51.

Haley, J. (1971). *The power tactics of Jesus Christ and other essays.* New York: Avon.

Hall, C. S., & Lindzey, G. (1978). *Theories of personality.* New York: Wiley.

Hanfmann, E. (1968). Angyal, Andras. In D. L. Sills (Ed.), *International encyclopedia of the social sciences, Volume 1* (pp. 302–304). New York: Macmillan & the Free Press.

Hebb, D. O. (1949). *The organization of behavior.* New York: Wiley.

Hebb, D. O., & Thompson, W. R. (1968). The social significance of animal studies. In G. Lindzey & L. Aronson (Eds.), *Handbook of social psychology, Volume 2* (pp. 729–774). Reading, MA: Addison-Wesley.

Hofstadter, D. R., & Dennett, D. C. (1981). *The mind's I.* New York: Basic Books.

Horowitz, M. (1988). Formulation of states of mind in psychotherapy. *American Journal of Psychotherapy*, 42, 514–520.

Janov, A. (1972). *The primal scream.* New York: Dell.

Jenkins, S. J., Stephens, J. C., Chew, A. L., & Downs, E. (1992). Examination of the relationship between the Myers-Briggs Type Indicator and empathetic response. *Perceptual & Motor Skills*, 74, 1003–1009.

Jourard, S. M. (1971a). *The transparent self.* New York: Van Nostrand.

Jourard, S. M. (1971b). *Self-disclosure.* New York: Wiley.

Jung, C. G. (1971). *The portable Jung* (J. Campbell, editor). New York: Viking.

Kasper, C. J., Baumann, R., & Alford, J. (1984). Sexual abusers of children. *Transactional Analysis Journal, 14,* 131–135.

Kelly, G. A. (1955). *The psychology of personal constructs.* New York: Norton.

Kohlberg, L. (1984). *Essays on moral development.* New York: Harper & Row.

Kolm, S. C. (1985). The Buddhist theory of 'no-self.' In J. Elster (Ed.), *The multiple self* (pp. 233–265). New York: Cambridge University Press.

Laborit, H. (1988). *L'agressivité d'etournée.* Paris: Union Général d'éditions.

Laing, R. D. (1967). *The politics of experience.* New York: Pantheon.

Laing, R. D. (1969). *The divided self.* New York: Pantheon.

Lecky, P. (1949/1969). *Self-consistency.* Garden City: Doubleday.

Lester, D. (1970). The concept of an appropriate death. *Psychology,* 7(4), 61–66.

Lester, D. (1975). The relationship between paranoid delusions and homosexuality. *Archives of Sexual Behavior,* 4, 285–294.

Lester, D. (1984). Systems theories of personality. *Psychology, 21*(1), 12–14.

Lester, D. (1985). Applications of the principles of group behavior to systems theories of personality. *Psychology,* 22(2), 1–3.

Lester, D. (1986). The rate of psychological functioning in theories of personality. *Psychology*, 23(4), 48–49.

Lester, D. (1987a). A systems perspective of personality. *Psychological Reports, 61,* 603–622.

Lester, D. (1987b). Systems theories of personality: implications from Boulding's writings. *Psychology,* 24(3), 44–46.

Lester, D. (1987c). The concept of integration in systems theories of personality. *Psychology,* 24(4), 66–67.

Lester, D. (1988). *The biochemical basis of suicide.* Springfield, IL: Charles C Thomas.

Lester, D. (1990a). An analysis of poets and novelists who completed suicide. *Activitas Nervosa Superior, 32,* 6–11.

Lester, D. (1990b). Maslow's hierarchy of needs and personality. *Personality and Individual Differences,* 11, 1187–1188.

Lester, D. (1992). The disunity of the self. *Personality & Individual Differences, 8*, 947–948.

Lester, D. (1993–1994). On the disunity of the self. *Current Psychology, 12*, 312–325.

Lester, D., & Thinschmidt,(J. (1988). The relationship of Laing's concept of ontological insecurity to extraversion and neuroticism. *Personality and Individual Differences, 9*, 687–688.

Leuba, C. (1955). Toward some integration of learning theories. *Psychological Reports, 1*, 27–33.

Lewin, K. (1935). *A dynamic theory of personality*. New York: McGraw-Hill.

Lewin, K. (1936). *Principles of topological psychology*. New York: McGraw-Hill.

Lifton, R. J. (1970). *History and human survival*. New York: Random House.

Loevinger, J. (1977). *Ego development*. San Francisco: Jossey-Bass.

London, P. (1964). *The modes and morals of psychotherapy*. New York: Holt, Rinehart & Winston.

Lundh, L. G. (1983). *Acta Universitis Upsaliensis: Number 10. Mind and meaning*. Uppsala, Sweden: University of Uppsala.

Lycan, W. G. (1981). Form, function and feel. *Journal of Philosophy, 78*, 24–50.

Maher, B. (Ed.), (1969). *Clinical psychology and personality: The selcted papers of George Kelly*. New York: Wiley.

Mair, J. M. M. (1977). The community of self. In D. Bannister (Ed.), *New perspectives in personal construct theory* (pp. 125–149). New York: Academic.

Margolis, H. (1982). *Selfishness, altruism and rationality*. New York: Cambridge University Press.

Maslow, A. H. (1942). Self-esteem (dominance feeling) and sexuality in women. *Journal of Social Psychology, 16*, 259–294.

Maslow, A. H. (1963). The need to know and the fear of knowing. *Journal of General Psychology, 68*, 111–125.

Maslow, A. H. (1968). *Toward a psychology of being*. Princeton: Van Nostrand.

Maslow, A. H. (1970). *Motivation and personality*. New York: Harper & Row.

McAdams, D. P. (1994). *The person*. Fort Worth, TX: Harcourt Brace.

McCawley, A. (1965). Exhibitionism and acting-out. *Comprehensive Psychiatry, 6*, 396–409.

McCulloch, W. S. (1965). *Embodiments of mind*. Cambridge, MA: MIT Press.

McReynolds, P. (1956). A restricted conceptualization of human anxiety and motivation. *Psychological Reports, 2*, 293–312.

McReynolds, P. (1960). Anxiety, perception and schizophrenia. In D. Jackson (Ed.), *The etiology of schizophrenia* (pp. 248–292). New York: Basic.

Meleshko, K. G. A., & Alden, L. E. (1993). Anxiety and self-disclosure. *Journal of Personality and Social Psychology, 64*, 1000–1009.

Menninger, K., Mayman, M., & Pruyser, P. (1967). *The vital balance*. New York: Viking.

Miller, G. A., Galanter, E., & Pribram, K. H. (1960). *Plans and the structure of behavior*. New York: Holt, Rinehart & Winston.

Minsky, M. (1986). *The society of mind*. New York: Simon & Schuster.

Mowrer, O. H. (1964). *The new group "therapy*. Princeton, NJ: Van Nostrand.

Mowrer, O. H. (1966). *Abnormal reactions or actions?* Dubuque, IA: W. C. Brown.

Murray, H. A. (1938). *Explorations in personality.* New York: Oxford.

Murray, H. A. (1959). Preparations for the scaffold of a comprehensive system. In S. Koch (Ed.), *Psychology, Volume 3* (pp. 7–54). New York: McGraw-Hill.

Murray, H. A., & Kluckhohn, C. (1953). Outline of a conception of personality. In C. Kluckhohn and H. Murray (Eds.), *Personality in nature, society, and culture* (pp. 3–49). New York: Knopf.

Myers, I. B., & Briggs, K. (1987). *The Myers-Briggs Type Indicator.* Palo Alto, CA: Consulting Psychologists Press.

Neimeyer, R. A. (1993). An appraisal of constructivist psychotherapies. *Journal of Consulting and Clinical Psychology, 61*, 221–234.

Ogilvy, J. (1977). *Many dimensional man.* New York: Oxford University Press.

Ouspensky, P. D. (1949). *In search of the miraculous.* New York: Harcourt, Brace & World.

Parsons, T. (1959). An approach to psychological theory in terms of the theory of action. In S. Koch (Ed.), *Psychology, Volume 3* (pp. 612–711). New York: McGraw-Hill.

Parsons, T. (1966). *Societies.* Englewood Cliffs, NJ: Prentice-Hall.

Pears, D. (1985). The goals and strategies of self-deception. In J. Elster (Ed.), *The multiple self* (pp. 59–77). New York: Cambridge University Press.

Perls, F. (1969). *Gestalt therapy verbatim.* Moab, UT: Real People Press.

Perls, F. S., Hefferline, R. F., & Goodman, P. (1951). *Gestalt therapy.* New York: Julian.

Peterson, D. R. (1967). The insecure child. In O. H. Mowrer (Ed.), *Morality and mental health* (pp. 459–471). Chicago, IL: Rand McNally.

Petrie, A. (1967). *Individuality in pain and suffering.* Chicago: University of Chicago Press.

Phillips, J. L. (1969). *The origins of intellect.* San Francisco: W. H. Freeman.

Piaget, J. (1960a). *The child's conception of the world.* London: Routledge.

Piaget, J. (1960b). *The psychology of intelligence.* New York: Harcourt Brace.

Pinker, S. (1994). *The language instinct.* New York: William Morrow.

Plutchik, R. (1962). *The emotions.* New York: Random House.

Progoff, I. (1973). *Jung's psychology and its social meaning.* Garden City, NY: Anchor, 1973.

Rapaport, D. (1959). The structure of psychoanalytic theory. In S. Koch (Ed.), *Psychology: The study of a science, Volume 3* (pp. 55–183). New York: McGraw-Hill.

Rogers, C. R. (1959). A theory of therapy, personality, and interpersonal relationships, as developed in the client-centered framework. In S. Koch (Ed.), *Psychology: The study of a science, Volume 3* (pp. 184–256). New York: McGraw-Hill.

Rogers, T. B. (1981). A model of the self as an aspect of the human information processing system. In N. Cantor & J. F. Kihlstrom (Eds.), *Personality, cognition and social interaction*, pp. 193–214. Hillsdale, NJ: Erlbaum.

Rohrer, J. (1952). A study of the predictive utility of the Role Construct Repertory Test. Unpublished doctoral dissertation, Ohio State University.

Rorty, A. O. (1985). Self-deception, akrasia and irrationality. In J. Elster (Ed.), *The multiple self* (pp. 115–131). New York: Cambridge University Press.

Rosenberg, S. (1993). Chomsky's theory of language. *Psychological Science, 4*, 15–19

Rowan, J. (1990). *Subpersonalities*. London: Routledge.

Sampson, E. E. (1983). Deconstruing psychology's subject. *Journal of Mind & Behavior, 4*, 135–164.

Scott, L., & O'Hara M. W. (1993). Self-discrepancies in clinically anxious and depressed university students. *Journal of Abnormal Psychology, 102*, 282–287.

Seyle, H. (1974). *Stress without distress*. New York: Lippincott & Crowell.

Shapiro, S., & Elliott, J. (1976). *The selves within you*. Berkeley, CA: Explorations Institute.

Shostrom, E. (Director). (1965). Three approaches to psychotherapy [Film]. Orange, CA: Psychological Films.

Sidgwick, H. (1893). *The methods of ethics*. London: Macmillan.

Southgate, J., & Randall, R. (1978). *The barefoot psychoanalyst*. London: Association of Karen Horney Psychoanalytic Counsellors.

Spiro, M. (1953). Ghosts. *Journal of Abnormal & Social Psychology, 48*, 376–382.

Steedman, I., & Krause, U. (1985). Goethe's Faust, Arrow's possibility theorem and the individual decision-taker. In J. Elster (Ed.), *The multiple self* (pp. 197–231). New York: Cambridge University Press.

Steiner, C. (1974). *Scripts people live*. New York: Grove.

Stice, E. (1992). The similarities between cognitive dissonance and guilt. *Current Psychology, 11*, 69–77.

Toman, W. (1960). *An introduction to the psychoanalytic theory of motivation*. New York: Pergamon.

Wagner, E. (1971). Structural analysis. *Journal of Personality Assessment, 35*, 422–435.

Watts, A. (1961). *Psychotherapy east and west*. New York: Random House.

Weakland, J. H. (1960). The "double-bind" hypothesis of schizophrenia and three-party interaction. In D. Jackson (Ed.), *The etiology of schizophrenia* (pp. 389–440). New York: Basic.

Weisman, A., & Hackett, T. P. (1961). Predilection to death. *Psychosomatic Medicine, 23*, 232–256.

Weiss, E. (1950). *Principles of psychodynamics*. New York: Grune & Stratton.

Werner, H. (1957). *Comparative psychology of mental development*. New York: International Universities Press.

Yalom, I. D. (1980). *Existential psychotherapy*. New York: Basic Books.

Zamansky, H. S. (1958). An investigation of the psychoanalytic theory of paranoid delusions. *Journal of Personality, 26*, 410–425.

Index